The Art of **SERIES**
EDITED BY CHARLES BAXTER

The Art of series is a line of books reinvigorating the practice of craft and criticism. Each book is a brief, witty, and useful exploration of fiction, nonfiction, or poetry by a writer impassioned by a singular craft issue. *The Art of* volumes provide a series of sustained examinations of key, but sometimes neglected, aspects of creative writing by some of contemporary literature's finest practitioners.

The Art of Subtext: Beyond Plot by Charles Baxter

The Art of Time in Memoir: Then, Again by Sven Birkerts

The Art of History: Unlocking the Past in Fiction and Nonfiction by Christopher Bram

The Art of Perspective: Who Tells the Story by Christopher Castellani

The Art of Intimacy: The Space Between by Stacey D'Erasmo

The Art of Description: World into Word by Mark Doty

The Art of the Poetic Line by James Longenbach

The Art of Daring: Risk, Restlessness, Imagination by Carl Phillips

The Art of Attention: A Poet's Eye by Donald Revell

The Art of Time in Fiction: As Long as It Takes
by Joan Silber

The Art of Syntax: Rhythm of Thought, Rhythm of Song
by Ellen Bryant Voigt

*The Art of Recklessness: Poetry as Assertive Force and
Contradiction* by Dean Young

THE ART OF HISTORY

UNLOCKING THE PAST IN
FICTION AND NONFICTION

Also by Christopher Bram

Surprising Myself
Hold Tight
In Memory of Angel Clare
Almost History
Gods and Monsters
Gossip
The Notorious Dr. August
Lives of the Circus Animals
Exiles in America
Mapping the Territory: Selected Nonfiction
Eminent Outlaws

The Art of

HISTORY

UNLOCKING THE PAST IN FICTION AND NONFICTION

Christopher Bram

Graywolf Press

808.056
BRA

7-1-16 HL

"Ghosts in the Details" first appeared in the *Yale Review*.
"Exhibit C: *War and Peace*" first appeared in *Commonweal*.

This publication is made possible, in part, by the voters of Minnesota through a Minnesota State Arts Board Operating Support grant, thanks to a legislative appropriation from the arts and cultural heritage fund, and through a grant from the Wells Fargo Foundation Minnesota. Significant support has also been provided by Target, the McKnight Foundation, the Amazon Literary Partnership, and other generous contributions from foundations, corporations, and individuals. To these organizations and individuals we offer our heartfelt thanks.

Published by Graywolf Press
250 Third Avenue North, Suite 600
Minneapolis, Minnesota 55401

www.graywolfpress.org

Published in the United States of America

ISBN 978-1-55597-743-6

2 4 6 8 9 7 5 3 1
First Graywolf Printing, 2016

Library of Congress Control Number: 2015953716

Cover design: Scott Sorenson

In memory of
Barbara Chalmers MacEdwards

Contents

3   "The Nearest Exit May Be Behind You"

17   Exhibits A and B: Two Tales

35   Ghosts in the Details

57   Lives and Other Stories

75   Exhibit C: *War and Peace*

85   The Macro and the Micro

105   Exhibit D: American Slavery

129   The Comedy of History

145   Endings

THE ART OF HISTORY

UNLOCKING THE PAST IN FICTION AND NONFICTION

"The Nearest Exit May Be Behind You"

When I was a sophomore in high school, I had an English teacher named Mrs. Comstock, a handsome, formal, forty-something lady with a stiff neck in a high collar. This was 1968 in Virginia Beach, Virginia, and she was already an anomaly, a throwback to an earlier age. But there was nothing stiff or formal about her love of books or the fearlessness with which she shared ideas with us. She spoke about the lack of tragedy in *Gone with the Wind* ("Scarlett O'Hara is not heroic"), the pain in Kafka ("Never read 'In the Penal Colony' while fixing dinner"), and the surprise of Theater of the Absurd (when a student asked for the point of a whole literature about meaninglessness, Mrs. Comstock replied, "What's the point of a whole literature about meaning?"). She read us Dorothy Parker ("Byron and Shelley and Keats / Were a trio of lyrical treats") and Lawrence Ferlinghetti ("Christ climbed down / from His bare Tree / this year"). Now that I'm a teacher myself, I'm in awe of both her energy and her willingness to share personal enthusiasms with a room full of sulky, college-bound overachievers. This was *superior* English. At the time I was delighted just to meet an adult who was so passionate about books.

One day she asked if anyone would like to live in

another time beside the present, and, if so, what would it be? I thought this was an excellent question but knew not to jump in too quickly for fear of looking weird. I was an eccentric, goofy kid with a big nose and glasses, a Boy Scout who loved to read. But nobody's hand went up. A few sheepish looks were exchanged, but no one said a word.

Finally I raised my hand. "I want to live in the seventeen hundreds."

Mrs. Comstock looked surprised. "Oh? That's one of my favorite periods."

I eagerly explained that I was reading *Northwest Passage* by Kenneth Roberts, the tale of a young artist who joins Rogers's Rangers during the French and Indian War and travels deep into the wilderness by canoe and foot. It was my idea of heaven.

Mrs. Comstock blinked a few times: this wasn't the eighteenth century she had in mind. (Later I learned that her eighteenth century was more along the lines of Voltaire's Age of Reason.) She turned to the rest of the room, however, hoping I had broken the ice. "Somebody else?" she asked. "Nobody? You're all so happy living in the present?"

More silence. Finally someone volunteered that they liked the present fine, thank you, and had no desire to live in a time before, uh, bathrooms. Everyone else nodded in agreement.

I was stunned. I had assumed most people loved the past as much as I did. It explained the shelves and shelves of history books at the library. It supported the popularity of time-machine stories, ranging from those of H. G. Wells to the cartoon adventures of Mr. Peabody and Sherman. But I was more alone than I thought.

Mrs. Comstock smiled at me, sighed sadly, and proceeded with the day's lesson.

The truth of the matter is that many people—maybe the majority—don't like the past very much. And it's not just anxiety about toilet facilities.

There is so much past, for one thing, so much history. It can be overwhelming. And the study of history is notoriously boring, with too many strange names and places and dates. All those different years and centuries are too much like math, and nobody likes math. For some of us the numbers alone are as evocative as colors, not just famous numbers, like 1492 or 1776, but more obscure, magical ones, like 1588 or 1832 or 1914. Yet for many readers these figures can be as forbidding as algebra. And that's not even taking into account ancient times, the BC dates, when time runs backward.

Then there are the people who are not only different from us but dry and serious, brutal and loveless. Jane Austen caught this resistance nicely when a character in *Northanger Abbey* says, "But history, real solemn history I cannot be interested in . . . The quarrels of popes and kings, with wars and pestilences, in every page; the men all so good for nothing, and hardly any women at all."

There's also the brutal public meaning of the word itself: *history* as a vast machine of politics and war that breaks into private happiness. "History is a nightmare from which I am trying to awake," says Stephen Dedalus in *Ulysses*, written during the First World War. To which the poet Delmore Schwartz responded decades later, during the Cold War, "History is a nightmare: during which I am trying to get a good night's sleep." Why think about this monster when you don't have to?

We don't always want to link the past and present. The past is more recent than we like to think. There is comfort in believing that the horror of Vietnam or the Holocaust or even segregation was long, long ago. I once caught an episode of *The Oprah Winfrey Show* in which she was talking with a handful of gay TV writers. Inevitably one of them compared the treatment of gay people to that of blacks in the age of segregation. A young white man in the audience protested, "But that was hundreds of years ago." Even Oprah was stunned. "No, it wasn't," she said sharply. It was easier for the young man to live with his country's crimes when he believed they'd happened once upon a time, in a very distant past.

And yet, and yet—there are many of us who love history and cannot visit it too often. We love it for different reasons. We like to believe it's good for us, but that's not why we are first drawn back in time. I believe history's original appeal is as pure escape. The past offers a fact-based fantasy, a dream with footnotes. Some people escape into the future of science fiction, but others prefer the past. As the flight attendants instruct us before takeoff, "The nearest exit may be behind you."

Look at *Northwest Passage.* This is the first grown-up novel that fully engaged me, taking me out of the trap of family life in the suburbs, into the freedom of green forests and rushing rivers in colonial America. Not only was it an escape into a new landscape and era for me, but it is a novel about escape, where its young narrator, Langdon Towne, flees the New England civilization of knee britches and churches (and a bad girlfriend) into the wilderness. It's not the Eden he expects, but what Eden ever is?

A more recent example is the novel *Wolf Hall* by Hilary Mantel. The tale of the rise of Thomas Cromwell during the reign of Henry VIII, it takes us out of our civilized present into an action-packed world of violence and intrigue wrapped in a fancy prose style. It's a ripping yarn, a literary cousin of the reimagined Middle Ages of TV's *Game of Thrones*. As daily life has become kinder and gentler, people seem to want their entertainment to be more brutal and sadistic. But maybe both *Hall* and *Thrones* aren't pure escapes after all: these dog-eat-dog tales suggest modern corporate life, only this time the backstabbing is done with real knives. It can be fun for frustrated office workers to see their not-so-secret fears and desires acted out at a safe distance as spectacle. (The inclusion of *Game of Thrones* here shows how close to fantasy history can get.)

A different example is the British TV series *Downton Abbey*. It offers an escape not only into the past but into wealth and privilege. It also takes us to a time when all men and women knew their "place." This is not the simple fantasy one might think. The class differences read more strongly for British viewers, but Americans, too, can't help enjoying life in an age when class resentments and fears were reduced and one's goals were simplified. You cannot feel like a failure for not being an earl when the position is only hereditary. I confess that I identify most strongly with the people downstairs, since their work comes closest to the life I know. (My favorite character is Mr. Carson, the gruff, stuffy, bulldog-faced butler: I wish I could be half as good at my job as he is at his.)

These escapes are not found just in fiction. The

reader can experience them in the grab bag of wonder tales about life in the West in Evan S. Connell's *Son of the Morning Star* or in the accounts of sixteenth-century voyages in Samuel Eliot Morison's *The European Discovery of America* or in the wry comedy of court life at Versailles in Nancy Mitford's *Madame de Pompadour.*

Orlando by Virginia Woolf offers a more profound kind of escape, not just from the present but also from the confines of a seventy-five-year life span. Woolf is a cosmic escape artist here, racing us and her sex-changing protagonist through four centuries, from Elizabethan horseback rides to a dizzying trip upward in a department-store elevator. This is the joy of time travel at its purest, where process is the protagonist and the contents merely happenstance.

We begin with escape, but we can't help learning things. We pick up idle bits of information while browsing through the encyclopedia of the past, fun facts to know. *Northwest Passage* first introduced me to the painters William Hogarth and John Singleton Copley: I knew them as "fictional" characters before I knew their work. One discovers all kinds of interesting odd and ends, ranging from medieval weaponry to Presbyterian church hymns to the evolution of the crinoline. This is the *Antiques Roadshow* side of history.

More important, the past increases our store of

stories. Story is our bread and butter here: tales, yarns, dramas, narratives. A curious assemblage of character, action, and emotion, a story can function as its own time machine, carrying the reader into another era. History provides more stories for writers as well as readers. As a novelist I'd be trapped with my own limited firsthand experience if I couldn't look elsewhere. I grew up to be a bookish gay man who leads a surprisingly small-town existence in the middle of New York City; I have been with the same partner for thirty-plus years. My world is pretty narrow. But by writing about the past, I can expand my range with research and imagination and educated guesswork, exploring life I'd feel unqualified to explore in the present. I may not know everything about Hollywood in the 1930s, but neither does my reader, and so I felt free to take my chances in my novel about movie director James Whale, *Father of Frankenstein.* Being white, I know nothing about being racially oppressed, but writing about a friendship between a young black man and a young white man in another era, the second half of the nineteenth century, in *The Notorious Dr. August: His Real Life and Crimes,* I was able to address poisonous experiences I've been spared.

Story is a wonderful elixir for readers, too. We can imagine ourselves in a much wider variety of roles in the past than we can in the confines of the present.

I can become not only a young American in a birch-bark canoe or a butler in an English country house but an eyewitness to the Battle of Borodino, or a slave in nineteenth-century Virginia, or a president of the United States. Story is the universal solvent in the pages that follow, the bridge between fiction and nonfiction, past and present. Any human experience should be accessible to story. David McCullough in *The Path between the Seas* makes the massive, complicated activity of building the Panama Canal as dramatic and involving as a long love affair. Toni Morrison renders the unthinkable thinkable in *Beloved* when she plunges us into the experience of slavery by exploring its scars on a free family.

This brings us to the more serious benefits of studying history. I really do believe visits to the past are good for us. History is good medicine. Just as Wittgenstein said we must study philosophy in order to protect ourselves from it, I believe we must study history to protect ourselves from its misuse. We need to confront the simple truth that the past isn't as long ago as we think, and it isn't radically different from the present. And we must learn to distinguish fact from fantasy. The American past is regularly distorted and abused by various spokespeople and politicians. This year I'm thinking in particular of the Tea Party wing of the Republican Party. They recently attacked the high school Advanced Placement tests for being too negative, i.e., for talking too much about slavery, labor wars, and the killing of Indians. A woman on Colorado's state board of education insisted we should celebrate the special virtues of our nation, such as the fact that we ended slavery "voluntarily." (She somehow forgot about the three-quarters of a million people who died in the Civil War.)

But members of the Tea Party can get awfully negative themselves when it suits their needs. They like to claim that the Founding Fathers wanted us to be a republic and not a democracy, and that we've lost our way as a result. What they really mean is that poor people shouldn't be allowed to vote. And, yes, our country began as a republic in which voter eligibility was limited by property, gender, race, education, and employment. But the Founding Fathers never did anything to stop the country from becoming more democratic in its first decades, and some, like Benjamin Franklin, actually worked toward it. (Of course, the Tea Partiers assume they will still be able to vote no matter what the restrictions might be.)

Such people believe that history offers a magical mystery solution to the problems of the present. It's the flip side of the fear of history that I began with. Those who think the past is a murky darkness are prey to crackpot theories about conspiratorial takeovers or

falls from grace. They feel that if only they can identify the single, fatal misstep or overlooked villain, they
will be able to explain *everything.* They read history in
much the same way they read the Bible—as a book of
secret codes and ironclad rules—and do not notice that
both are slippery, contradictory, living documents.

Often by escaping our present we see it anew, from a
distance. We face it with fresh eyes. We see the bigger picture. History can enable us to place ourselves
in time, offering a way to see the world more clearly,
as if from a mountaintop or even the moon. Goethe
wrote, "A person who does not know the history of
the last 3,000 years wanders in the darkness of ignor-
ance, unable to make sense of the reality around
him." I think Americans are doing pretty good if we
know the past 300 years—bringing us back to colonial times.

As we grow older, more and more of us want to
visit the past. We overcome our fear and boredom.
I'm not sure why. Perhaps we just grow more curious. Or maybe it's because we have enough private
past of our own that we feel confident we can keep
our heads above water in the flood of time. And so we
visit the past in different ways. We do it through historical novels, which can range from the soft romance
of Georgette Heyer to the acerbic satire of Gore Vidal

to the leisurely westerns of Larry McMurtry. Or we do it through popular history, a misnomer that sounds like substandard history but only means history with a strong narrative. It includes work by literary journalists like McCullough but also by serious scholars like Edmund Morgan, Brenda Wineapple, and John Demos, who've written conventional analytic history but were drawn to storytelling. We also visit the past in film documentary, a new form that triumphed on PBS with Ken Burns and his brother Ric Burns and other filmmakers but has continued in recent decades with a score of fine visual storytellers who know how to use old photos, voice-overs, and music to create fact-based dreams. There is a growing hunger for all kinds of vital, relevant, entertaining pieces of time past.

Much can be gained by treating fiction and non-fiction as different sides of the same mountain. Their similarities and differences can instruct us about how we read history and write it, and how we think about it as well. And they are not as different as one might think. Unlike historians, novelists are free to make up some of their facts, but it's a relatively minor point. Those "facts" must feel solid and established. The reader needs to believe that the story already exists and that neither the historian nor the novelist is inventing anything but is simply choosing which facts to include and in what order. If a novelist changes his mind about his story and breaks faith with it, the reader will suffer the paradoxical thought, "Why, they're just making it up as they go along." There are exceptions, of course, occasions when a novelist wants to change the rules. But most novels aspire to the condition of history.

Exhibits A and B: Two Tales

Let's begin with two books, one a historical novel, the other a work of narrative history. We can look at an artist working as a historian and a historian working as an artist. I've chosen two books whose worlds stand next door to each other in time and location but are universes apart in terms of their subjects.

We don't think of Gabriel García Márquez as a historical novelist, but much of his work is set in the past or in a past that soon bleeds into the present. The choice of verb is deliberate. García Márquez writes about a region that has suffered too much history—in the brutal meaning of the word. He revels in the phantasmagoria of history, the dream of it—or nightmare. His most famous novel (one of the most famous novels of the twentieth century), *One Hundred Years of Solitude*, presents history as a nightmare from which the author is trying to awake. War takes over the middle of the book, a blow to the head that creates a concussion of story fragments and broken characters. It's a tornado of a novel, in which hundreds of indistinguishable events are whirled around and around. García Márquez includes no dates—time, too, is broken—but students of

Colombian history recognize the War of a Thousand Days (1899–1902) and the Ciénaga massacre (1928). More than one member of the Buendía family stands in front of a firing squad. The book strives to be an escape from emotion, an escape from pain. The characters are as flat as playing cards, and the novel suggests a long card game in which the author changes the rules whenever he likes. There's a deliberate weightlessness at work.

However, his later novel, *Love in the Time of Cholera*, is full of weight and emotion. This is the highly romantic tale of unrequited love, a love that lasts for decades.

Again García Márquez avoids dates, leaving us stranded in time. (Nor does he tell the name of the old Caribbean city where the novel takes place, though it appears to be a mix of Barranquilla and Cartagena in Colombia.) But there are chronological signposts. In a prologue set on Pentecost Sunday, we're told a new movie, *All Quiet on the Western Front*, played the night before in the open-air theater of a ruined convent, setting us in 1930. It's a busy day for Dr. Juvenal Urbino. He signs the death certificate for a friend who committed suicide with cyanide. A colleague at the hospital gives a party. Dr. Urbino is eighty-one; his wife, Fermina, is seventy-two; they have children and grandchildren.

The opening takes place in the leisurely once-upon-a-time of another era—a poor country can't help having the timelessness of a folk or fairy tale. Yet García

Márquez includes odd historical details that place it in an identifiable past: horse-drawn carriages and automobiles, scented pomade and celluloid collars, old studio photos of children "startled by the magnesium flash." The prologue is dominated by a malevolent yellow-headed parrot who struts around the house, lewdly chuckling to itself. It speaks French and Latin and mimics the songs of Yvette Guilbert and Aristide Bruant from Dr. Urbino's phonograph. The doctor is a Francophile, and the performers are relics of the Paris of Toulouse-Lautrec in the 1890s. This overly articulate bird is the literal death of the doctor: he falls from a ladder while trying to catch it.

After the funeral, the grief-stricken Fermina finds a lean, bony old man standing in the empty parlor. "Fermina," says Florentino Ariza, "I have waited for this opportunity for more than half a century, to repeat to you once again my vow of eternal fidelity and everlasting love." Then we leap back in time to 1870, when poor young Florentino fell in love with thirteen-year-old Fermina, only to lose her to Dr. Urbino.

The 1930 prologue accomplishes several things. First, it declares that Florentino will not win Fermina in the main body of the novel; the suspense of *what* is replaced by the mystery of *why*. But it also deepens and complicates the past. The past has its own past. No age is purely itself but is colored with ghosts and shadows, just like the present. The prologue also enables us to enter the past more slowly, step by step, so we don't suffer the historical equivalent of future shock.

This is a novel of love stories, endless love stories; they come one after another or are stuffed inside each other. Florentino's love for Fermina doesn't stop him from falling in love with other women. "My heart has more rooms than a whorehouse," he declares. It's a fairy-tale novel full of real emotional toads. Depending on whose side you take, Fermina is a bitch or Florentino is a pest. Yet García Márquez sympathizes with all his lovers. Married love is given the same weight as romantic love, and Fermina's long marriage to Dr. Urbino is presented as detailed, changing, and real.

> They had just celebrated their golden wedding anniversary, and they were not capable of living for even an instant without the other, or without thinking about the other, and that capacity diminished as their years increased. Neither could have said if their mutual dependence was based on love or convenience, but they had never asked the question with their hands on their hearts because both had always preferred not to know the answer.

I believe *Love in the Time of Cholera* is a more mature, wiser, stronger novel than *Solitude.* García Márquez is bitter and flippant when he writes about war and politics, understandably so. He has no sympathy for that world, or pity, either. Writing about love, however, frees him to feel more deeply. He is not afraid to be gentle. The chaos of love doesn't overwhelm and numb him the way that the chaos of war does. (But people still get hurt. One of Florentino's lovers, a fourteen-year-old girl named America, will commit suicide with laudanum.) Love enables García Márquez to explore time more slowly and carefully than war does. Time is his other great subject.

He began the novel as the imagined tale of how his own parents met. He did much research, but the information is digested in the strong emotion and humor of the story. Magical realism is replaced by an exaggerated but plausible cartoon realism. Dr. Urbino returns home from France on a ship that passes through "a floating blanket of drowned animals." During Fermina's trip through the mountains, a string of mules falls into a ravine, and "the screams of the man and his pack of seven animals tied to one another continued to rebound along the cliffs and gullies for several hours after the disaster, and continued to resound for years and years in the memory of Fermina Daza."

The occasional bodice-ripper quality is transformed by playful parody into a kind of poetry. The language is always elegant and shapely, old-fashioned in its formality yet unafraid to include "a tender breath of human shit, warm and sad." (García Márquez is not shy about toilet facilities.) It's the prose of telling rather than showing, but the rule "Show, don't tell" doesn't always apply when we are engaged in storytelling.

The book gains much by being set a hundred years ago. It gives the characters room to breathe, a place for sixty years of unrequited longing to unfold. It's also an age when people still believed one could die of love. The trope feels more plausible in the late nineteeth century than it does today, a lost piece of human behavior, like dueling or fainting. The novel is one long argument with the "tragedy" of unrequited love.

García Márquez uses history primarily as a setting for a love story. By adding the missing dates, I've made *Love in the Time of Cholera* more like a work of history than the author intended. But García Márquez also tells us much about the past. We see the modernization of Latin America over sixty years, the coming of new technologies, the shifts of class, the rise of poor men like Florentino into money and property. It's a world as well observed as the worlds of *Buddenbrooks* or *The Magnificent Ambersons.* The civil wars and atrocities of *Solitude* are regularly mentioned, but they take place offstage and never threaten the protagonists. However, we do see the new age destroy the environment in the course of two journeys by steamboat on the Magdalena River. During the first, Florentino travels upriver to escape the city where his beloved Fermina is marrying Dr. Urbino. The riverscape is lush and green, the trees full of parrots and monkeys, the water full of maternal manatees. When he returns at the end of the novel, the forests have been cut down for fuel; the parrots, monkeys, and manatees are dead.

Florentino has resumed his courtship of the widowed Fermina and finally won her. After a cascade of love letters written on that unromantic invention, the typewriter, the elderly couple reunites on a riverboat that Florentino owns.

> It was as if they had leapt over the arduous calvary
> of conjugal life and gone straight to the heart of love.
> They were together in silence like an old married
> couple wary of life, beyond the pitfalls of passion,
> beyond the brutal mockery of hope and the phan-
> toms of disillusion: beyond love. For they had lived
> together long enough to know that love was always
> love, anytime and anyplace, but it was more solid the
> closer it came to death.

Wanting to be alone, they ask the captain to fly the cholera flag. It's 1932, and the epidemics promised by the title are actually a thing of the past, but a yellow quarantine flag isolates the pair as they travel up and down the dying river in a *Heart of Darkness* of requited love.

David McCullough is a very different kind of writer. I like to think that this is the first time he and García Márquez have ever appeared on the same page. McCullough is respected as a historian and enjoyed as a storyteller, but he is too often taken for granted—perhaps because he makes what he does look so easy.

McCullough is a remarkable craftsman with a gift for matching form with subject. In *The Great Bridge* he uses the construction of the Brooklyn Bridge as the spine for a series of tales about engineering, New York City politics, and Victorian America—the bridge supports the book just as the newly invented suspension cables support the bridge. In *Mornings on Horseback,* he restricts himself to the early years of Theodore Roosevelt to create an intimate account of the man and his parents. *Truman* gives us the life of Harry Truman chronologically, a more traditional womb-to-tomb story. The book starts out as the quiet chronicle of a decent, down-to-earth middle-American everyman. But a third of the way in, Everyman is made vice president to FDR, the wartime president who will soon die. An element of suspense enters the story and stays with the book for its next six hundred pages as crisis follows crisis, a roller coaster of events that shows Harry is a tougher, more competent, more soulful man than anyone could have expected.

The Path between the Seas is another kind of history, a complex epic about the building of the Panama Canal. The scale of the book matches the scale of its subject. It incorporates a remarkable range of stories, from tales of adventure and exploration to financial chicanery out of *The Way We Live Now* by Anthony Trollope to the imperialist politics of *Nostromo* by Joseph Conrad to medical discoveries worthy of *Nova*. And then there's the great dig itself. This is a saga that ups the ante on what was achieved in *The Great Bridge*. McCullough takes his time laying out these plots and pulling them together. The book itself is an impressive feat of narrative engineering: you can feel McCullough digging steadily through the layers of story with the same tenacity as the men digging the canal.

It's a difficult subject to make human. There is a cast of hundreds, many of whom are little more than names who offer a few words or actions before they depart, a revolving chorus of soldiers, engineers, bankers, diplomats, politicians, lawyers, middle-class revolutionaries, and doctors. McCullough tells us just enough about each to make them distinct. Two world-famous figures, the charismatic French financier Ferdinand de Lesseps and the equally charismatic American president,

Theodore Roosevelt, are present, but they're just part of this lively, teeming crowd.

Panama is two hundred miles west of the unnamed city of *Love in the Time of Cholera* and was originally a province of Colombia. Like *Cholera,* this book begins with a prologue, a detailed account of the French attempt to build the canal from 1881 to 1888. There are expeditions and surveys, banquets and conferences, plans and counterplans. The geography is presented piecemeal until, a hundred pages in, we get the vivid report of a six-hour train trip across the isthmus, from the Atlantic to the Pacific, by de Lesseps and his coterie. The setting is laid out for us with wonderful reality: the flooded Chagres River, the rain forests and mangrove swamps, the pass at Culebra, the harbor of Panama City. This extended prologue is actually the first act of a three-act play. It fills the first third of the book, introducing the landscape and geology, the technology, and the deadly antagonists yellow fever and malaria. It also offers an alternate story to the American tale of triumph told later. The French tale ends with mass graves and rusty machinery overgrown by jungle.

In addition to his gift for story construction, McCullough has an eye for the telling quote. He writes excellent prose himself and can even give life to that tired standby of popular history, the weather:

The skies, when it was not raining, were nearly always filled with tremendous, towering clouds—magnificent clouds, and especially so in the light of early morning. Then there would be an unmistakable rush of wind in the trees, a noticeable drop in temperature, a quick darkening overhead followed by a sound that someone likened to the "trampling of myriad feet" through the leaves. In villages and towns everyone would instinctively dash for cover. From the hills at Culebra the jungle could be seen to vanish before onrushing silver cataracts of rain, and howler monkeys would commence their eerie ruckus.

The French are defeated not by the jungle or disease or even their decision to build a sea-level canal instead of a canal with locks, but because their company is badly underfinanced. The prologue ends in a flurry of investor meetings and stock panics, followed by charges of corruption and blackmail fed by the new anti-Semitism, the mysterious death of a banker, and the sensational trials of de Lesseps and his son Charles. As Thelma Ritter's character says in *All about Eve,* "Everything but the bloodhounds snapping at her rear end."

A new phase opens. We shift from the French belle époque to the first decade of what would be known as the American Century, a brighter age of white suits and dresses and Teddy Roosevelt. There is another round of banquets and speeches—it was an age of banquets—and quarrels over whether the canal should be in Panama or Nicaragua. Backroom deals and financial shenanigans resume—the Americans are no better here than the French. McCullough treats these maneuvers without scorn or indignation. He is surprisingly sunny for a historian, tending to be positive about character and generous about motive. Like García Márquez, he can be funny, yet there's less bitterness underneath. He's no Pollyanna but a worldly realist. Self-interest is a given fact of human nature, and he is never shocked by the idea that men do things for money. He counters the black-and-white melodramas of journalism with a more complicated view in which the villains are rarely as bad as they're painted and the heroes always more human. (His generosity may be why *John Adams* doesn't entirely work for me—the only book by McCullough about which I can say that. He avoids the irascible man's dark side and leaves out his anger altogether. The book becomes, as a biographer friend says, "a long walk on level ground.")

When Colombia hesitates over a deal in 1902 to cede a swatch of Panama to the United States for only ten million dollars, Roosevelt declares its leaders no better than bandits. (McCullough shows more understanding of and respect for the Colombian government than either Roosevelt or García Márquez does.)

A handful of middle-class Panamanians organize a quiet revolution, aided by a lawyer in New York and a French engineer-adventurer. The Americans promptly recognize the new country of Panama, which gets the ten million dollars. Latin America will never trust the United States again.

Now begins the third act, the actual construction of the canal. There are still delays and complications. The first American year is a fiasco, marked by a yellow-fever panic and aimless digging. Two protagonists appear in the crowd of characters. Dr. William Gorgas, the army medical chief, overcomes the resistance to "the mosquito theory" (already proved by Walter Reed in Cuba) and combats yellow fever and malaria with fumigation and drainage. A new chief engineer, John Stevens, reorganizes the project, improves the infrastructure, and persuades the Senate to approve a lock canal instead of a sea-level canal. By 1906 more than twenty-four thousand workmen are toiling in the fifty-mile-long corridor.

The book picks up momentum; the last hundred pages are an energetic narrative of work and technological know-how. President Roosevelt visits during the rainy season and is famously photographed sitting in a ninety-five-ton Bucyrus steam shovel. He takes equal delight in both "orchids and steam shovels." The trip mirrors de Lesseps's visit at the beginning of the book, but the story is nowhere near finished. There will be two more presidents, Taft and Wilson, and a new chief engineer—colorless, efficient, lonely George Goethals—before the canal is completed.

McCullough includes a full-scale portrait of the American colony during construction, a middle-class utopia that suggests *Meet Me in St. Louis* transported to the tropics—a utopia for whites, anyway. Life is far more difficult for the black West Indians who make up three-quarters of the workforce. There are also many paragraphs of first-rate technical writing, precise descriptions of reinforced concrete or new electrical motors or the construction of the cathedral-sized locks that are like glimpses into the future.

Toward the end McCullough provides a wonderful set piece about the excavation at Culebra Cut, the man-made canyon cut through nine miles of rock.

> Panoramic photographs made at the height of the work gave an idea of how tremendous that canyon had become. But the actual spectacle, of course, was in vibrant color. The columns of coal smoke that towered above the shovels and locomotives—"a veritable Pittsburgh of smoke"—were blue-black turning to warm gray; exposed clays were pale ocher, yellow, bright orange, slate blue, or crimson like that of the soil of Virginia . . . The noise level was beyond belief.

He quotes a company journalist's description of the spectacle: "a swarming mass of men and rushing railway trains, monster-like machines, all working with ceaseless activity, all animated seemingly by human intelligence, without confusion or conflict anywhere." Yet the book has made clear that "without confusion or conflict" was only an illusion.

The first ship steams through the canal from the Atlantic to the Pacific on August 15, 1914. Festivities planned for the grand opening are canceled due to the start of the First World War, two weeks earlier.

The echoes between *Cholera* and *Path* are striking, and not only because they take place in the same region and era. McCullough's sensuous description of a rainstorm would not be out of place in García Márquez's novel. There are no fully developed love stories in *Path,* but one could imagine a character in *Cholera* behaving as a French engineer does in *Path:* the man grieves so deeply over the death of his wife from yellow fever that he takes the family's prize horses into the mountains and shoots them. The fatal diseases that are a metaphor in the novel are murderously real in the history book.

There's a similarity of voice, a third-person omniscient narration that is slightly old-fashioned but appropriate for both history and historical fiction. García

Márquez's prose is more playful, of course, while McCullough's is sprinkled with facts and figures. The two writers take their time, letting the plots and subplots unfold steadily, although the novelist will sometimes leap ahead with brief remarks about the future. We've already seen the similarities of structure: one needs to build a nonfiction narrative with the same care and cunning that one uses with a novel.

But the differences are just as striking. First there is the sheer number of characters in *Path*, like that swarming mass of men and machines seen at Culebra Cut. Historian Steven Runciman wrote that "a historical canvas is necessarily crowded, and readers who are afraid of crowds should keep to the better-ordered lanes of fiction." Novelists have tried complicated sagas equal to what McCullough achieves, but not even *The Way We Live Now* or *War and Peace* comes close. No novelist's imagination can match the invention, superfluity, and utter wastefulness of actual history.

Cholera has many supporting characters but only three protagonists. It is, after all, a bundle of love stories. Novels are often love stories. "A small tale, generally about love" was Samuel Johnson's old definition of *novel* before books like *Clarissa* showed how big a love story could be. Many novelists burn to write about something else, but love remains our chief subject. And we do love much better than historians or even biographers, whether it's romantic love, married love, family love, or friendship.

History books usually work on a much smaller scale than *The Path between the Seas,* but group life still looms larger than private life. The divide between group life and private life will come up later when we talk about Tolstoy—Tolstoy will appear more than once in this book. Novels tend to be about private individuals wandering in the mystery of history. Most nonfiction history and biography are about active individuals who interact with other active individuals and produce that mystery—and don't always understand it any better than the civilians.

People never tire of saying that truth is stranger than fiction. But that's because fiction needs to mean something, while true events can simply be. True stories speak to us most strongly when they mean something, too.

Both *Cholera* and *Path* have happy endings, but their achieved goals could not be more different. After many years two lovers finally find each other. After endless trials and defeats, a new world power drives a shortcut between two oceans. We're more likely to fall in love and get married than we are to build something like the Panama Canal. Nevertheless, I think readers can get meaning and wisdom from both of these books. In one we intimately experience love in the rush of years and the shadow of death. In the other we witness that rare thing, a great public project that is about peace, not war, a real-life answer to William James's call for heroic action that is "a moral equivalent of war." It's more distant, less personal, more abstract than love, but spectacles can offer their own lessons.

Ghosts in the Details

"The past is a foreign country," L. P. Hartley famously wrote in *The Go-Between:* "they do things differently there." So it's no surprise that good history writing often resembles good travel writing. We read travel books for the anomalies and surprises of other countries and cultures. We want to see things that are different and see them vividly. We visit the past in much the same way. Difference enables us to see things more intensely. If things are too different, however, we can't connect or respond. Make it strange, we say, but not too strange.

We experience this historical difference most keenly through details, the odd objects or striking moments or alien bits of behavior that snap another world to life. Details are the raisins in the raisin bread. Story is the bread. Let's begin with the raisins.

Here's a brief sample of memorable details from history, biography, and novels:

- The opening page of *The Leopard* by Giuseppe Tomasi di Lampedusa presents an aristocratic family kneeling in prayer. The outward piety and formality, like a nineteenth-century group portrait, evoke Sicily in 1860. Then we read: "The women rose slowly to their feet, their oscillating skirts as they withdrew baring bit by bit the naked figures from mythology painted all over the milky depths of the tiles." In one sentence we see the period clothes, the old palace, and the contradictory inner life.

- Arthur Schlesinger in *The Coming of the New Deal* mentions that FDR preferred not to wear his bridgework but always put it into his mouth before he gave his Fireside Chats on the radio; otherwise he hissed his *s*'s.

- *Memoirs of Hadrian* by Marguerite Yourcenar is written in a voice so close to the Roman emperor that the past dissolves into timelessness. But now and then odd details plunge us back into the past, as when he tells us about the trials of public speaking in the rain. "Protected only by my toga, which caught the water in its gutter-like folds, I had to continually wipe the rain from my eyes as I pronounced my discourse. Catching cold is an emperor's privilege in Rome, since he is forbidden, regardless of weather, to put anything over the toga."

- Mary Beth Norton's account of the Salem witch trials, *In the Devil's Snare*, includes details missing in most other accounts. Townspeople begin to dream of witches, and their visions—feasts of red bread, a yellow bird nursing at a witch's finger, an animal familiar with the head of a bird and body of a lion—sound less like Puritan New England and more like images from Bosch.

- Tolstoy declares in the first chapter of *War and Peace* that his upper-class Russian characters frequently use French, "the elegant tongue of our grandparents, who used it for thought as well as speech." (A recent translation feels this isn't enough strangeness and insists on presenting those conversations in French—even though Tolstoy himself put them in Russian in later editions.)

- Samuel Eliot Morison pauses in his encyclopedic *The European Discovery of America* to tell us that wine stored by the Greeks and Vikings in wineskins (with the hairy side facing in) had a distinctly gamey taste.

- Virginia Woolf's *Orlando* includes two glorious pages on the coming of the nineteenth century as a cloudy, fertile dampness that produced ivy, babies, and the British Empire. The damp even "gets into the inkpot as it gets into the woodwork—sentences swelled, adjectives multiplied, lyrics became epics, and little trifles that had been essays a column long were now encyclopedias in ten or twenty volumes." Pure fantasy, of course, but nobody who's read

those pages will ever think of Victorian England in
the same way.

- *Son of the Morning Star* by Evan S. Connell includes
the story of a man named William Thompson who
survives his own scalping—it sounded from inside
like "bubbles or blisters popping"—and rides home
on a train with his scalp floating in a bucket of
water.

And so on. Some details are more trivial than others.
They can be physical, social, or psychological, yet all help
us enter the foreign country of the past. They mix the
familiar and the strange. They work through surprise,
but also through precision, word choice, and humor.
Most good writing is built out of details, of course,
small strokes of observation, little shocks of recogni-
tion. It's said that the devil speaks in generalizations,
but God is in the details. I don't know about God, but
there are definitely ghosts in historical details, and ghosts
can be useful in storytelling.

Details, specifics, particulars are what many of us
enjoy most when reading history. They are illustrations
in the text. They are what we remember. Their importance becomes clear in books where they are absent or
few. Steven Runciman writes clear, crisp, elegant sentences about the thirteenth-century Mediterranean in
The Sicilian Vespers, but one reads desperately from

page to page, hungry for another "human interest" moment such as when the Byzantine emperor is murdered in his bath with a stone soap dish.

But not all details are good. There are research details, period details, which are just data from the past and not terribly interesting in themselves. There is pleasure in recovering old things from the junk shop of history, but an overload of period details can clog a narrative. Tolstoy uses surprisingly few, which is one reason why *War and Peace* remains alive. He tosses them in now and then when they are needed. George Eliot piles on the data in her historical tales, so that *Romola,* her Renaissance novel, and even *Adam Bede,* set in the late eighteenth century, can be a chore for modern readers. This is the Reverend Mr. Irvine's dining room in *Adam Bede:*

> The room is a large and lofty one, with an ample mullioned oriel window at one end; the walls, you see, are new, and not yet painted; but the furniture, though originally of an expensive sort, is old and scanty, and there is no drapery about the window. The crimson cloth over the large dining-table is very threadbare, though it contrasts pleasantly enough with the dead hue of the plaster on the walls; but on this cloth there is a massive silver waiter [a tray] with a decanter of water on it, of the same pattern as two larger ones

that are propped up on the sideboard with a coat of arms conspicuous in their center.

It's not without interest, but not everyone wants to wade through a Sears and Roebuck catalog to get to the story.

In most successful books about history, fiction and non-fiction, the story is in the foreground and the details are neatly woven into it. They're hard to pull loose. But let's cheat and look at a couple of books where the details dominate.

The Leopard by Lampedusa is all details, and good details, too. There is a plot, but it floats just beneath the surface like a submerged wreck. This is a historical novel where all the history takes place offstage, just as it does in the lives of most readers. Set in the early 1860s during the Risorgimento, the reunification of Italy, the book tells the story of Fabrizio Corbera, Prince of Salina, the forty-five-year-old head of a large, wealthy family with palaces and estates in different parts of Sicily. Known as the Leopard, *il gattopardo*, after the family crest, the Prince represents the old order, yet he is not the dinosaur we expect. He is intelligent, curious, open-minded. He is aware of the changing times, but he doesn't fight them. He doesn't join the change, either, although he's in partial sympathy with it. He encourages his nephew,

Tancredi, to become part but remains detached himself. He serves as a remarkable conduit for ideas and emotions about the losses and gains of history.

The movie made from the novel by Luchino Visconti is excellent, faithful to its unconventional shape and exquisite feeling for detail. Yet even a great movie can only scratch the surface of the inner life the prose renders so beautifully. Lampedusa concentrates not on story but on individual days, much as Tolstoy and Turgenev did in their work. (V. S. Pritchett discussed this approach in his lovely essay "The Russian Day," where he explored how loose and inclusive a single day can be. "In all those Russian novels we seem to hear a voice saying: 'The meaning of life? One day that will be revealed to us—probably on a Thursday.'") *The Leopard* takes place during a handful of days scattered over three years. Two chapters at the end look into the future. Drama, emotion, and ideas are revealed in details presented over the course of each day.

The first chapter covers twenty-four hours, from afternoon prayer to afternoon prayer, in the main estate outside Palermo. There is a "disturbance" in the city—a revolt against the Austrian rulers—whose meaning the Prince understands all too well. But he goes on with his daily routine, which includes dinner with his family, a visit to a prostitute, a meeting with tenants, and an astronomy session with Father Pirrone, the family priest. Pirrone is ostensibly the spiritual master, but he is dependent on the Prince for his livelihood. He carefully balances his duty to God with what he owes his short-tempered employer. The two men disagree about politics, don't agree entirely on religion, yet both love astronomy. In a few pages Lampedusa gives us a complicated, layered relationship that is both foreign and recognizable.

After the liberation of Palermo by Garibaldi (which Lampedusa lightly skips over), the Salina family travels by caravan to their palace in Donnafugata, a dusty town in a treeless region of the interior. The Prince is a feudal lord here, and he worries about how he'll be treated after the recent political changes. The family is received with the usual pomp in the town square. The first new note is that the town band plays selections from *La traviata*, the most recent opera of the new nation's musical hero, Verdi. Even the organist in the church performs a piece from this tragic tale of a Paris courtesan. The world is clearly shifting. Outside the church, the Princess invites the local dignitaries to dinner that evening. There is doubt over whether or not the men's wives are dignified enough to be included. But the Prince intervenes and invites the wives, too:

> And he added, turning to the others, "And after dinner, at nine o'clock, we shall be happy to see all our

friends." For a long time Donnafugata commented on these last words. And the Prince, who had found Donnafugata unchanged, was found very much changed himself; for never before would he have issued so cordial an invitation: and from that moment, invisibly, began the decline of his prestige.

It's a wonderfully simple moment, the shift from feudal order to democratic free-for-all, expressed in a thoughtless gesture of good manners.

"If we want things to stay as they are, things will have to change," Tancredi tells the Prince early on. It becomes a mantra for the novel, a justification for the changes that will gradually change everything.

The change is all in little dramas, never big ones. Tancredi courts the daughter of the mayor, a former peasant with a fortune. The Prince votes for unification in a local plebiscite but is disgusted when the mayor declares the vote unanimous—he knows several men who voted against it. Nevertheless, he surrenders his nephew to the daughter of a man he now calls a jackal. An emissary from Turin visits and invites the Prince to join the new government as a senator. The Prince refuses in a strange, fatalistic, revealing speech about the vanity and insularity of Sicilians. "I'm sorry; but I cannot lift a finger in politics. It would only get bitten." The next day, he tells his visitor good-bye and adds, "We were the Leopards and Lions; those who'll take our place will be little jackals, hyenas; and the whole lot of us, Leopards, jackals and sheep, we'll all go on thinking ourselves the salt of the earth."

The novel is both a pastoral and an elegy, the beautiful evocation of a paradise that's appealing for modern readers even as we see the seeds of its paralysis and demise. And it's all revealed not in high dramas but by well-chosen details.

Details are usually used more sparingly in nonfiction history, but Connell's *Son of the Morning Star* is a treasure house of detail. Connell assumes we all know the basic story of Custer's Last Stand, the great American symbol of white hubris and Indian justice, and he turns his attention to the mountains of anecdotes he discovered in diaries, letters, memoirs, court transcripts, and old history books while researching the massacre. *The Leopard* is told chronologically, which makes it easier to sense the story hidden underneath. Connell dispenses with chronology and presents his anecdotes with their own helter-skelter order. They are more vivid than they'd be if embedded in a conventional narrative.

He opens in the middle of the story, in medias res: "Lt. James Bradley led a detachment of Crow Indian scouts up the Bighorn Valley during the summer of 1876." The reader already knows what these men will find in this rolling, treeless landscape, but Connell takes his time, letting what's known become a mystery again. Bradley and his men see something in the distance. Several paragraphs later they report what they find.

> Lt. Bradley returned from the other side of the river to say that the dark objects on the hillside thought to be buffalo skins were, in fact, dead horses. What had been mistaken for skinned buffalo carcasses were the naked bodies of Custer's men. Bradley had counted 197 dead soldiers. This news paralyzed the advancing army. A mule packer in Roe's company, Pvt. William H. White, said that for a quarter of an hour there was very little talking.

Story leads to story, digression to digression. From one page to the next, the book feels shapeless, but it has just enough structure under this fluid surface to feel solid. After the discovery of the massacre, Connell gives an account of Reno's unit, which survived. (Reno attacked the Little Bighorn village from the east while Custer attacked from the north. Reno fled and was pinned down by the Indians for three days.) Then he loops back to short bios of Reno and his men, a life of Crazy Horse, tales of Indian life, tales of army life, flashbacks to the Civil War, flash-forwards to the twentieth century, and a full-scale portrait of George Armstrong

Custer and his wife, Libby. Finally he gives us the event at the center of the story, the slaughter of Custer and his men. Withholding that key scene holds the book together with the suspense of waiting for the other boot to drop.

Connell was a novelist before he became a historian, the author of several fine books, including two crisp, quiet novels about his family, *Mrs. Bridge* and *Mr. Bridge.* He was always an inventive, unconventional writer with a keen appreciation of the anomalies of human behavior. In *Son of the Morning Star,* he regularly pursues any interesting tale that catches his interest, even if it's not immediately relevant to the whole. He sometimes gives contradictory versions of the same anecdote, but not so many that we become lost. The book is like a jigsaw puzzle where most of the pieces have been laid out but not yet fitted together—including many extra pieces. It's a rare page that doesn't contain something worth noting or quoting. Here are Reno's men describing the withdrawal of the Sioux and Cheyenne after three days of fighting:

> One member of H Company, Charles Windolph, recalled many years later: "The heavy smoke seemed to lift for a few moments, and there in the valley below we caught glimpses of thousands of Indians on foot and horseback, with their pony herds and

travois, dogs and pack animals, and all the trappings of a great camp, slowly moving southward. It was like some Biblical exodus; the Israelites moving into Egypt; a mighty tribe on the march." Lt. Edgerly felt less poetic: "I thought before the ponies commenced to move that it was like a lot of brown underbrush; it was the largest number of quadrupeds I ever saw in my life . . . It looked as though a heavy carpet was being moved over the ground."

We see the scene vividly in the twin points of view, as if in a pair of binoculars looking back through 140 years.

Here is Custer's own account of his first ride in an observation balloon during the Civil War:

The basket in which we were to be transported was about two feet high, four feet long, and slightly over half as wide, resembling in every respect an ordinary willow basket of the same dimensions, minus the handles. This basket was attached to the cords of the balloon. Stepping inside, my assistant, after giving directions to the men holding the four ropes, told me to take my place in the basket. I complied, and before being fully aware that such was the fact found that we were leaving *terra firma,* and noiselessly, almost imperceptibly, ascending toward the clouds . . . The interstices in the sides and bottom [of the basket]

seemed immense, and the further we receded from
the earth the larger they seemed to become, until
I almost imagined one might tumble through.

Any man who can tell such a story could not have been
a complete idiot.

The book shouldn't work, but it does, carrying the
reader with its deadpan narrative voice and remarkable wealth of material. The vivid details cut through the
myths and clichés to make the story new and strange
again. And the myths are now part of the story and
Connell incorporates them, too, including the gory
1896 Anheuser-Busch lithograph of the battle that hung
in saloons across the country for decades. (One still
hung in my local barbershop in Norfolk, Virginia, in
the 1950s, when I was a small boy. I remember staring
at it in morbid fascination every time I got a haircut.)

When the big battle scene finally arrives at the end
of the book, Connell continues to sketch with multiple
overlapping lines and erasures, producing a picture of
a world in motion. Events are now told entirely from
the viewpoints of the Cheyenne and Sioux, of course;
the whites were all killed. The fight lasted less than
a half hour. "The Americans went down like sheep,
Rain [in the Face] said. It was as easy as killing sheep."
The last word is given to a Cheyenne woman named
Kate Bighead, who told her story in sign language to

a white doctor in 1927. The women, children, and old men all watched from a nearby ridge, but Kate Bighead got much closer. She saw the soldiers firing at Indians they couldn't see while thousands of arrows fell from the sky, sticking in horses and the backs of men. She did not learn until later that the soldiers were led by the notorious Custer. "I have often wondered if, when I was riding among the dead where he was lying, my pony may have kicked dirt upon his body." Those are the final words of the book, a small, surprising, perfect note at the end of this sprawling epic.

The best details in a work of history, fiction or nonfiction, are like double knots of character and time: they tie us to both the people and the age they live in. Think, for example, of the ball in *The Leopard* when the melancholy Prince waltzes with beautiful young Angelica and "at every twirl a year fell from his shoulders; soon he felt back at the age of twenty, when in that very same ballroom he had danced with [his wife] before he knew disappointment, boredom and the rest. For a second, that night, death seemed to him once more 'something that happens to others.'" Few of us know fancy dress balls or even how to waltz, but all of us can recognize the Prince's state of mind. In the middle of endless killing at the end of *Son of the Morning Star* is a moment of slapstick. A warrior named Iron Hawk sees a soldier play dead while two old women strip him. When they start to castrate him, the naked man jumps up and swings them around as if dancing. Iron Hawk still found the story funny when he told it years later. The comedy makes all the participants recognizably human, which makes the experience more horrifying.

How does a writer find the right details? Through research, of course, but a loose, daydreamy, haphazard kind of research. You immerse yourself in the period you're writing about, reading history, memoirs, and novels. Period novels are especially good, but so are old newspapers, illustrated catalogs, and visits to museums and antiques shops. You explore mostly to put yourself in the mood, building an inner reality like a method actor. But you begin to notice particular anomalies and quirks that bring the past to life *for you*. You trust that they will bring it alive for other readers, too. Sometimes you can use these discoveries whole. Other times you must forget them and rediscover them all over again in your imagination.

For example, years before I wrote a novel set in nineteenth-century New York, *The Notorious Dr. August,* I read Anthony Trollope's book about his visit to the city in 1862, *North America.* It is full of strange odds and ends, but the most vivid is Trollope's hatred of crinolines. He was obsessed with the fashion for enormous skirts spread over elaborate hoops and wires.

He complained that they took up space in omnibuses and hallways and that he was always stepping on the hems and runners. I forgot about his account until I was writing about my narrator's childhood in a small house full of women in the 1860s. I remembered those crinolines and I wanted to include them, but without going on at length like Trollope. I did it in one sentence: "Their enormous balloon skirts squashed through doorways and whistled against the wallpaper." The sound and sense brought the period to life in my mind in all its strangeness; I hoped it would do the same for some readers. But it also expressed Fitz's feeling of claustrophobia as a child, the fear that he was being crowded out of his own home.

The best details do the double duty of evoking both a character and an age. But there are also profound details that do triple duty, offering a glimpse into something larger, the society or religion or philosophy of the time. They are harder to achieve and tend to be unexpected inspirations or happy accidents.

Not all details work, of course. Sometimes they get in the way. Readers want the writer to make it strange, but not too strange. Too much strangeness can be distracting. Some historians and biographers like to give quotes in their original archaic spellings and capitalization to emphasize their pastness. But Victoria Glendinning, in her fine biography of Jonathan Swift, modernized the spelling and explained why in the preface: "Period flavor can be just too intrusively flavorsome. You might object that this is as perverse as saying 'Hold the mayo' when ordering lobster mayonnaise. But I would rather give proper attention to the lobster."

What succeeds and what fails can be very subjective. *Wolf Hall* by Hilary Mantel is written almost entirely in period details in close-up, a bold experiment that works for some readers but not for me. Striving for immediacy, the novel is all present-tense moments with the context deliberately left out. What remains is a brilliant, woozy, Joycean surface of robust prose, but the novel often feels like it's all lobster mayonnaise and no lobster. For example, a boy named Tom is brutally beaten by his father in the first pages. We never learn why.

> Blood from the gash on his head—which was his
> father's first effort—is trickling across his face. Add to
> this, his left eye is blinded; but if he squints sideways,
> with his right eye he can see that the stitching of his
> father's boot is unraveling. The twine has sprung
> clear of the leather, and a hard knot in it has caught
> his eyebrow and opened another cut.

In the next chapter a man named Thomas serves a cardinal. Only the twenty-year difference in the dates of the chapter headings suggests the boy has become the man. Unlike García Márquez, Mantel includes dates, or the reader would be completely lost. But this isn't dream history, like *One Hundred Years of Solitude.* It's a complicated tale of conspiracy and power under Henry VIII; we need to know what's going on. Thomas is Thomas Cromwell; the cardinal is Cardinal Wolsey. Soon the cardinal is expelled from his palace, but we don't learn why for another sixty pages. (His failure to annul Henry's marriage to his first wife.) It helps if you know the history, or have at least seen *A Man for All Seasons,* but even then all is confusion and chaos. There's no room to breathe or to feel any emotion. The reader learns nothing new about history or human nature. Bad men are bad. The masses are fickle. It's the anti–*Man for All Seasons,* and Thomas More is a nasty shit, but I already knew that from an excellent biography, *Thomas More* by Richard Marius, which tells the story much better. (Marius shows that the man who was famously willing to die for his beliefs was a persecutor of heretics who was willing to kill for those beliefs, too, a harder concept for modern readers.) I wonder if Mantel's frantic, flashy style is the best way to tell any story, and there are still two more volumes to go.

Nevertheless, the book became a best seller. Well, some readers enjoy feeling dizzy, as if after a stiff drink. And it's heady, brutal stuff, a *Game of Thrones* for highbrows. But compare *Wolf Hall* with *The Fifth Queen* by Ford Madox Ford, another trilogy, written almost a hundred years earlier—before Ford wrote *The Good Soldier.* Also set in the reign of Henry VIII, but a few queens further down the road, this novel features Thomas Cromwell again, but in a secondary role. It, too, is full of Shakespearean dialogue, dense prose, and striking details, but Ford regularly mixes long shots and medium shots with his close-ups so that readers always know where they are. It may be slightly more old-fashioned than *Wolf Hall,* but I find it more accessible. And his details open windows into the characters, their age, and their beliefs. Mantel's details open windows only onto her own virtuosity. (The later TV adaptation of *Wolf Hall* is more accessible than the book, since the frantic, flashy prose is gone, but all we get is a poky costume drama full of gloomy actors muttering their lines with downcast eyes.)

Talk of details brings us to the role of facts in narrative history—or what people call truth. In nonfiction things need to be true, of course. You can change emphasis or interpretation, but you cannot claim that the Battle of the Little Bighorn took place on a different date than June 25, 1876, or that Custer won and Sitting Bull was killed. You can't present as fact a conversation that is totally invented.

But in fiction it's more slippery. Here there's enormous pleasure in making up stuff and convincing your reader it's real. There's the authority that comes with voice and surprise. The big bogeyman in fiction is anachronism, the wrong detail that can break the dream and throw us out of the narrative, but this is more subjective than it might seem. For example, a fluorescent light in a 1939 working-class home on the second page of *The Amazing Adventures of Kavalier and Clay* by Michael Chabon will startle only readers who happen to know that fluorescent lights didn't become cheap and commonplace until after World War II. First chapters are important because the reader is not yet so caught up in the story that he or she doesn't notice wrong notes. A strong narrative can sweep us past a host of trivial errors. And errors are inevitable. Writers can't always distinguish commonplace devices and language of time past from those of their own age. Yet these errors aren't as serious or destructive as many fear. It's all make-believe anyway. Writers just hope we're not so wrong that the dream is broken.

A more profound anachronism is the fallacy of "presentism," the assumption that the past is just like the present and the inner lives of humans remain the same from one century to the next. The past really is a foreign country. No writer can underestimate the rigid roles of race, class, and gender in other eras. Nobody can forget the hardness of life in the past or the power of religion. But I believe that it's equally wrong, and dangerous, to treat other ages as completely Other. If that were true, we'd be unable to feel any connection with Greek tragedies or Shakespeare's plays or even Victorian novels. They would be opaque mysteries to us. I believe the past is different but similar enough for us to see ourselves reflected there, like a fun-house mirror in which our experience and psychology are duplicated with fresh proportions, revealing distortions and strange, expressive shapes. We see ourselves new in the fun-house mirror of history.

Lives and Other Stories

Story is a wonderful way to organize experience. First one thing happens, then another and another. Events unfold in time and are connected by cause and effect, anticipation and suspense. Best of all, people are involved, individual men and women, which always makes the action more interesting.

There are many kinds of stories we can tell about the past. Let's begin with biography, because it has the simplest plot: a person is born, accomplishes something, and dies. Between the second and third stage, there are usually complications. Now and then someone writes a biography of someone who accomplished little, as Jean Strouse did in *Alice James,* about the brilliant invalid sister of Henry and William James, but Strouse is the exception who proves the rule.

Biography is its own continent, of course, with its own rules and pantheon. I discuss it here only as a subdivision of history and a sibling of the novel. Biography spills into the novel in the form of fictional biographies. The earliest novels include biographies and autobiographies of imaginary people: Robinson Crusoe, Moll Flanders, Tom Jones, and Tristram Shandy. Fictional bios are often about people who accomplish nothing.

Once there was something called the Great Man theory of history, in which superhuman world-class figures steered mankind in new directions. I don't think anyone believes that anymore, especially those who read biographies. We might read biography looking for villains and plausible heroes, but not for superheroes. And we read in hopes of understanding the world a little better. Biography does an excellent job of making complicated events more accessible by presenting them from one person's point of view.

Take the life of a figure everybody knows: Benjamin Franklin. All right, maybe people know only the stock image of the nice old man with stringy hair, granny glasses, and a kite. But we can go to a short, smart biography by Edmund Morgan, *Benjamin Franklin,* and see his entire life unfold as a story. Morgan was a serious historian who wrote this book late in his career. Others had written fat, "definitive" biographies of Franklin, so Morgan felt free to tell the story in a brisk three hundred pages.

He gives us Franklin's pre-political years quickly: He fled his apprenticeship with his brother in Boston, went to Philadelphia, set up his own business, and got married. He was athletic as a young man, a strong swimmer, but, like many athletes, his muscle turned to fat as he got older. His chief traits of mind were established early on: his self-control; his constant curiosity, which led to his experiments in electricity and heat; his discreet deism—he believed in God but not in Jesus or churches. He retired from printing when he was only forty-two, not wanting to get richer but needing to give himself to public service. He believed so strongly in public service that he refused to take out patents on his inventions, the lightning rod and the Franklin stove; he wanted everyone to benefit without profit to himself. He was one of the most sociable men imaginable, a poor public speaker but good in conversation and a keen listener.

Politics did not fully kick in for Franklin until 1750. He originally supported the British Empire, believing the differences between the colonies and the home government could be worked out to the benefit of both. But after the Stamp Act crisis, the government grew harsher and more inflexible. Franklin was criticized in a public hearing in London in 1774 "in language too coarse for newspapers to print." He listened in stoic silence. He did not give up on Britain until a year later, becoming a revolutionary at the ripe age of sixty-nine. He returned to Philadelphia in time for the Declaration of Independence, then went back to Europe, where he negotiated the alliance with France and later the peace treaty with Britain. He was in Philadelphia again for the drawing-up of the Constitution, in 1787, three years before his death, at age eighty-four. Throughout it all, he listened, organized, offered advice, and wrote droll articles and perceptive letters. (He said of John Adams, "He means well for his Country, is always an honest Man, often a Wise One, but sometimes and in some things, absolutely out of his Senses.")

Franklin was a late bloomer who kept blooming. He accomplished not just one thing but many things; his life is a thread that connects a remarkable number of historical dots. Through him the reader can experience firsthand the country's shift from thirteen obedient colonies to thirteen rebel states to a loose confederation to the United States. I haven't read a dull biography of him yet, but Morgan tells the tale with wonderful brio and verve. As with a symphony transcribed for the piano, it's easier to take in the whole when a man's life is laid out as simply and sharply as it is here.

A very different kind of life story is told in *Harriet Jacobs: A Life* by Jean Fagan Yellin. This is the tale of someone who was unknown until Yellin discovered the identity of the former slave who wrote *Incidents in the Life of a Slave Girl.* The memoir was published under a pseudonym in 1861, and the tale is so strange—a young woman hides in her grandmother's attic for *seven years*—that modern scholars suspected it was a novel written by a white abolitionist. But Yellin followed a few clues and discovered the true identity of "Linda Brent."

She learned that Jacobs wrote *Incidents* herself and that
the tough, direct prose is actually her voice.

> Why does the slave ever love? Why allow the tendrils
> of the heart to twine around objects which may at
> any moment be wrenched away by the hand of vio-
> lence? When separations come by the hand of death,
> the pious soul can bow in resignation, and say, "Not
> my will, but thine be done, O Lord!" But when the
> ruthless hand of man strikes the blow, regardless of
> the misery he causes, it is hard to be submissive. I did
> not reason thus when I was a young girl. Youth will
> be youth.

The unnamed town was Edenton, North Carolina,
and the hard-hearted Dr. Flint was a real man named
Dr. James Norcom. Yellin is even able to name Jacobs's
white lover, the father of her son and daughter. Good
Victorian that she was, Jacobs was deeply ashamed of
having children out of wedlock, which was why she used
a pseudonym.

More important, Yellin also gives us the rest of
Jacobs's life, from the 1842 escape north to her years
with the abolitionist movement to her work after the
war as a schoolteacher of the children of freed slaves.
She and her daughter owned their own boardinghouse
in Washington and another in Cambridge. But in the

Reconstruction years, she lost her property and her status, ending as a hired cook before her death, in 1897. This biography gives us a vivid history of black life before and after the Civil War—its successes and ultimate failure—through the life of one remarkable woman.

Fictional biographies are slightly different animals. The writer is usually (but not always) drawn to real-life people yet is free to mix imagination with research, filling in the gaps with invention, fleshing out barebone facts with colors and details.

Burr by Gore Vidal is the fictional life of Aaron Burr, one of the great dark enigmas of American history, a man who served heroically in the American Revolution, was vice president under Thomas Jefferson, shot Alexander Hamilton in a duel, and was accused of conspiracy after an attempted land grab out West. He can be seen as the Bad Fairy to Franklin's Good Fairy of the Early Republic. Vidal uses the ingenious device of a brilliant, world-class cynic, old Burr, telling his life story to a young cynic-in-training, Charlie Schuyler. We get two first-person narrators. It doesn't really matter that the real Burr wasn't nearly as smart and entertaining as Vidal's version of him—the real Burr cared more about money than about anything else. The double-cynic narrative enables Vidal to produce mocking portraits of Washington, Jefferson, and Hamilton that are half-joke, half-real, and always entertaining. It also helps Vidal dramatize the pastness of the past. In a very real New York City of the 1830s, Burr discusses events that took place forty years earlier. The distance between the two pasts magnifies things, much like the two lenses set a foot apart in a telescope.

An excellent example of this comes when Burr—known as the Colonel, due to his rank in the Revolution—takes Charlie across the Hudson to show him where he shot Alexander Hamilton. They row across the river alone and climb the cliff to the scene of the crime, and Burr reenacts the duel. Charlie narrates.

> The ledge is about six feet wide and perhaps thirty to forty feet long with a steep cliff above and below it. At either end a green tangle of brush partly screens the view of the river.
>
> The Colonel indicates the spires of New York City visible through the green foliage. "That is the last sight many a gentleman saw."
>
> I notice he is whispering. He notices, too, and laughs . . . "Just before seven o'clock Hamilton and his second Pendleton and the good Dr. Hosack—Hamilton was always fearful for his health—arrive. Just down there." Burr points. I look, half-expecting to see the dead disembark. But there is only river below us.

We are in an 1833 present, looking back at 1804, with Burr talking us through the duel, moment by moment, pistol shot by pistol shot. Burr insists that Charlie stand where Hamilton stood. Charlie is understandably shaken. It's far more effective than if Burr had simply narrated the events or Charlie had imagined them.

Another fine scene is when Burr visits Jefferson at Monticello. While they talk about racial inferiority and the slave revolt in Haiti, Burr notices the family resemblance of Jefferson's slaves. "It was a curious sensation to look about Monticello and see everywhere so many replicas of Jefferson . . ." The novel was published long before the DNA evidence convinced most historians that Jefferson really did father children with his slave Sally Hemings. Vidal was having fun with an insolent joke, but one with bitter truth in it. Fictional biographies are able to fill in gaps that factual biographies must treat either with silence or very tentative guessing. Almost all Vidal's additions are plausible and interesting. His account of the conspiracy that led to Burr's trial for treason is more engaging and easier to follow than the historical account by Henry Adams. His portraits of the Founders are prejudiced but always lively and memorable.

The Unreal Life of Sergey Nabokov by Paul Russell is another novel about a real person, but someone we know very little about: the younger brother of the novelist

Vladimir Nabokov. The paucity of information forced Russell to invent even as it liberated him from facts. I had a similar experience when I wrote my novel about James Whale, *Father of Frankenstein.* Necessity is not only the mother of invention; it gives us permission to make things up.

Like *Burr, Unreal Life* narrates from one past into another. Here the protagonist himself tells his story from the vantage point of Berlin in 1943. The Allied bombings and scarcity of food give a special sharpness to Sergey's memories of luxury, first love, sex, ballet, and opium in tsarist Russia and 1920s Paris. By themselves they'd be too rich, like a meal of chocolates. But in the context of wartime Berlin, they become appealing, even poignant.

Sergey is a rich gay boy who grows up in the shadow of an older, smarter, favored, heterosexual brother. He tells his story in lush, playful, often Nabokovian prose. For example, he remembers watching Vladimir, nicknamed Volodya, and a cousin bathe naked with their horses in a river one summer when he was twelve.

> The horses watched, tails flicking, as my brother and cousin waded out into the river till the water reached mid-thigh. Volodya's flesh was sun-toasted, Yuri's pale as milk . . . It was only my brother and my cousin, but in the afternoon light they seemed agents of some heavenly dispensation.

The adult Sergey is able to find words the young Sergey lacked to describe his sexual awakening. His account of the Russian Revolution, the family's poverty in Berlin, and the assassination of their beloved father is more frank and real than what Vladimir wrote about the experiences. Through Sergey, Russell recovers the horrors of history that Nabokov deliberately hides in most of his work. The novel is an imaginary triumph for the younger brother. But this half-real, half-imagined life is closed off in an epilogue with the brutal fact of Sergey's death from typhus in a concentration camp outside Hamburg.

Homosexuality is one area where fiction can complete what history, until recently, could only begin. The subject was taboo and the record sparse. But Mary Renault was able to flesh out—literally—the same-sex love of the ancient Greeks in such novels as *The Last of the Wine* and, gaudier and more exotic, *The Persian Boy.* Doris Grumbach took us inside the lives of the mysterious eighteenth-century "spinster" couple known as the Ladies of Llangollen in her novel *The Ladies.* There is a hypothetical what-if at the center of these books, an educated guessing at details, yet these men and women make more sense when their missing sexuality is included than when it was left blank.

Once we leave the relative simplicity of biography, it's harder to define the types of stories we can tell about history. The possibilities are extensive for fiction, but they seem endless in nonfiction. We can write about building projects like the Panama Canal, military campaigns like the Little Bighorn, political campaigns, natural disasters, financial collapses, crimes, trials, epidemics, bloody revolts, bloodless revolutions, the scribbling of books, and the fall of empires. In short, writers tell stories about any historical event or cluster of events that can be given a beginning, a middle, and an end.

A second important type of story is the mystery. The basic detective plot is as useful in history as it is in fiction. What happened? Why? Who did it? (Or for many readers: "Who's to blame?") Usually the historian is silent about his or her sleuthing, discussing it only in the introduction or footnotes, as Jean Fagan Yellin does in *Harriet Jacobs*. But sometime it is placed front and center, as C. Vann Woodward did in his investigation of the Compromise of 1877, *Reunion and Reaction,* where he unravels the deal that gave the deadlocked 1876 election to Rutherford B. Hayes. *The Affair of the Poisons* by Anne Somerset explores a rash of poisoning and witchcraft in the court of Louis XIV. Every biography of T. E. Lawrence, "Lawrence of Arabia," is also a detective novel, the author out to solve this enigmatic man. Who was he, really? Was he a hero or a fool, gay or straight, a con man or a saint?

Fiction uses the mystery plot more nakedly. In fact, there are several popular detective series set in the past. Steven Saylor's Gordianus the Finder investigates crimes in Rome at the time of Cicero *(Roman Blood, A Murder on the Appian Way)*. The Brother Cadfael novels by Ellis Peters *(One Corpse Too Many, The Devil's Novice)* look into murders in twelfth-century England. The William Monk novels by Anne Perry *(The Face of a Stranger, A Dangerous Mourning)* explore evil in Victorian London. Detective novels are constructed out of endless meetings and interviews. In a historical setting, this ritual enables the protagonist (and the author) to explore different aspects of the age: class, money, politics, custom, superstition, honor. Historical research disguised as the investigation of a crime becomes an important part of the action.

Probably the most famous example is *The Name of the Rose* by Umberto Eco. The novel is set in a monastery in 1327, and the detective is the logic-chopping know-it-all Brother William of Baskerville. His name connects him to Sherlock Holmes (Holmes is echoed in Gordianus the Finder as well), which is meant to be funny, and maybe it is, but in the leaden manner of jokes from an old-school philosophy professor. The repetitious, tortoise-paced narrative is meant to parody medieval scholasticism, but it gives the reader surprisingly little in the way of striking details or involving story from one chapter to the next. I get more fun, and a sharper picture of the Middle Ages, when Brother Cadfael investigates how King Stephen hanged ninety-four men for treason and ended up with ninety-five corpses.

A third type of story might be called the storyless story. Sometimes history fails to provide a plotline with which the historian can tie together the material and ideas he or she has gathered. So the writer produces a portmanteau book, a grab-bag book like *The Fabulous History of the Dismal Swamp Company* by Charles Royster. The title is a red herring. This eccentric, entertaining history is a loose collection of tales and anecdotes about men who invested in a land company in Virginia before the American Revolution. The company lasted from 1763 to 1814, but the tales spill in all directions. Page by page, Royster provides enough pieces of story to engage us, but he constantly slides off in new directions. This is a shaggy-dog history. It's a little like *Son of the Morning Star,* except where Connell dances away from his central narrative, there's no trace of any kind of narrative behind Royster's quick, sharp prose and amazing research. Instead of a plot, we get choice tidbits about land-poor Virginians, unfinished mansions, the South Sea Bubble, bills of exchange, an ambitious clerk who marries his boss's widow and disowns her children, the voyage of the slave ship *Hope,* smuggling in Antigua, the slave trade on the Gold Coast, the underwriter rooms of Lloyd's, theatergoing in London, bankruptcy, death, contested wills, and more marriages than one can keep track of. It's a history of the transatlantic world as imagined by Borges, and it drives some people crazy. A reader on Amazon complained that it was like reading through old account books, which I think is true and part of its charm. We are left free to dream of the life behind the inky columns of profit and loss.

I can think of no historical novels that use this rummage-sale approach, but there are contemporary novels that do, such as *Life: A User's Manual* by Georges Perec, where we get nearly a hundred different lives bound together by nothing but the fact that they all live in the same giant apartment building in Paris. You don't get a story, but you do get an atmosphere and a world, and that is enough.

Sometimes there is not enough story to sustain a book. And sometimes there are not enough facts to sustain a story. Here is where novelists usually step in. But some imaginative historians keep to the rules of evidence while filling the gaps with hypotheticals, creating hybrids of fact and imagination. There is much use of *maybe, perhaps,* and *possibly.* There is a lot of educated guessing. A loose net of subjunctives is thrown over a dark space in hopes of catching the outline of truth. James Shapiro does this very well in *A Year in the Life of William Shakespeare*, sketching in 1599, when Shakespeare seems to have written *As You Like It* and *Hamlet.* Claire Tomalin does it expertly in *The Invisible Woman,* her life of Ellen Ternan, the mistress of Charles Dickens, who deliberately wrote herself out of the public record.

This kind of responsible invention is especially necessary when dealing with people whose lives aren't normally recorded in history: the poor, the working class, minorities, and women. A fine example is *The Ordeal of Elizabeth Marsh* by Linda Colley, which follows an Englishwoman from one continent to another during the eighteenth century. We know a little about her shipwright family but a lot about her time in Morocco from her short book, *The Female Captive,* about when she and her future husband were captured by Barbary pirates and held hostage in Marrakech. We know nothing about her years in England but something about her time in India. Marsh may have been of mixed race, but we can't be certain. We have no portrait of her. Her letters have disappeared. Even her grave is gone. Her picaresque life suggests a real Moll Flanders, but she traveled more widely and seems to have been more virtuous than Defoe's heroine.

Colley lays out all the evidence that's available, admits where we know nothing, makes a guess here and there, and sometimes fills in the blank spaces with pieces from other people's stories. For example, Marsh left no record of her mastectomy in Calcutta, in 1785, but Colley quotes the harrowing description from novelist Fanny Burney's diary of her own operation, in 1811. Colley fills other blank spaces of Marsh's life with descriptions of the towns or seaports where she lived. We get a series of landscapes *without* a figure, a world populated by an absence. We often seem to arrive in a place just after Elizabeth Marsh has left it. Yet the rumor of her presence remains, and it is enough to keep us reading. We finish the book with a faint sense of Marsh but a very strong sense of her world. Colley admits in her conclusion:

> Resurrecting this obliterated life has been absorbing. It has also been challenging. More even than is true of the generality of biographical subjects, there is no possible owning of all the facts of Elizabeth Marsh's existence. Some of her life-parts, like her bones, like her image, are gone forever.

Novelists have learned from these unknowable stories. Novelists know everything, of course, or they can if they want to—after all, it's their story. But sometimes, in the name of verisimilitude, they claim to be ignorant. Joseph Conrad, in the voice of Marlow, isn't sure if Lord Jim is five foot ten or five foot eleven. Truman Capote claims not to know what happened to Holly Golightly at the end of *Breakfast at Tiffany's*. Novelists often leave holes in their tales to make them seem more real.

Novelists and historians constantly learn from each other. Historians want to make their stories as vivid as fiction; novelists want to make theirs as complex and original as history. It's said that there are only four different plots in fiction—or seven or twelve or fourteen or what have you. The number changes depending on who's making the list. Whatever the case, there seem to be a limited number of plotlines that novelists can use. But when they turn to history, they find variations and combinations and whole new animals they couldn't invent on their own. "You can't make this up," people like to say, almost as often as they say, "Truth is stranger than fiction." But you *can* make it up—only history often does it better.

Exhibit C: *War and Peace*

Some people dismiss historical fiction as a bastard genre, the lowly love child of history and romance. They forget that the book frequently cited as the greatest novel ever written is a historical novel. *War and Peace* is the gold standard of historical fiction as well as a classic of world literature. Sooner or later we must talk about *War and Peace.*

Leo Tolstoy wrote a historical novel that feels so immediate and natural that many people assume he was writing about his own time. They forget the book was published in 1869 and was about his parents' generation. Fictional versions of his father and mother actually appear in the novel: Nikolay Rostov and Marya Bolkonsky. They play a smaller role than García Márquez's parents do in *Love in the Time of Cholera,* but their presence is still important, a private ladder that enabled the author to climb down into time.

We think of *War and Peace* as a vast novel, but that's only in page length—1,358 pages in the Anthony Briggs translation. It actually covers only eight years, 1805 to 1812, with an epilogue. (Well, *two* epilogues, but that's a story for later.) I don't understand people who feel intimidated by it, put off by the length or rumors of difficulty.

The book is long, but it moves quickly, and the prose isn't nearly as complex as that of, say, *Middlemarch.* What adds to the novel's size are the enormous number of characters (but no more than in Dickens or Trollope) and the fact that Tolstoy takes few short-cuts. Here and there he leaps ahead in time or summarizes a few months of activity. But for the most part the book unfolds in day-to-day routines, producing the illusion of real life in real time. He doesn't overdo the period details. He locates events in the past with gentle reminders, such as his observation that this generation spoke French or a mention of stockings and knee britches or his quoting bad jokes told by society people. (Nothing dates like a bad joke.) He includes plot devices and scenes from an earlier age of romantic fiction—a deathbed struggle over a will; a duel with pistols; the attempted abduction of a young girl at night—but then puts them in the matter-of-fact "modern" language of the rest of the book.

War and Peace is much easier to summarize than one might think: it's not a densely plotted novel. At the center are two friends: handsome, melancholy Prince Andrey Bolkonsky and fat, bumbling, bespectacled Count Pierre Bezukhov. They express two different attitudes toward life: a stern, masculine distrust and a childlike, sometimes buffoonish openness. Their experiences form two parallel narratives that run through the entire novel.

Andrey serves in the military in the Austerlitz campaign against Napoleon. Pierre remains in Russia, where he inherits great wealth and ends up in a bad marriage. There's a third narrative, about the Rostov family, a happy, careless pack of aristocrats that includes a young officer, Nikolay, and his lovely, lively little sister, Natasha. Over the course of the novel, Natasha grows from an eager child of twelve into a serious woman of twenty. Andrey and Pierre both fall in love with her.

The two men define the book so strongly that it's a surprise to realize afterward that we see them together only three times. They meet first at the opening party scene. Later, between the wars, they meet in the country and compare their hopes and disillusion. Pierre, who has recently become a Freemason, argues that one must live for other people. Andrey counters that people can live only for themselves. They have one last meeting, on the eve of Borodino, but all Andrey can talk about is military strategy.

Andrey is the saddest character in a novel with a surprisingly high proportion of happy people. Even his religious sister Marya is content. Before Austerlitz, Andrey believes military glory can cure his existential despair. After Austerlitz and the death of his wife, he feels nothing can save him. One spring, riding in a carriage to the Rostov estate on a business matter, he passes a grove of birch trees in full leaf. In the middle stands an old oak tree that looks dead and broken. He identifies with the oak. At the estate he sees Natasha for the first time, a black-haired, black-eyed sixteen-year-old girl in a yellow print dress running with her friends in a field. That night he overhears her and her cousin chatting and singing at the window above his window. The moonlight is so beautiful, she wants to fly up into the sky. Andrey is charmed.

A week and three short pages after he first sees the oak, Andrey passes the birch grove again.

> "That oak-tree, it was somewhere near here in the forest. There was such an affinity between us," he thought. "But where was it?" As he wondered, he glanced across left and, unconsciously, without recognizing it, began to admire the very tree that he was looking for. The old oak was completely transformed, now spreading out a canopy of lush, dark foliage and stirring gently as it wallowed in the evening sunshine . . . "No, life isn't over at thirty-one," was his instant, final and irrevocable conclusion. "It is not enough for me to know what is going on inside me. Everybody must know about it—Pierre, and that girl who wanted to fly up into the sky—they must all get to know me. My life must be lived for me but also for other people."

Pierre experiences revelations like this every fifty or so pages, but they are very rare for Andrey. He goes to Petersburg and begins reform work for the government. He is soon disappointed. But on New Year's Eve, 1809, he attends the imperial ball and sees Natasha again, the girl he barely knows. They dance, and Andrey begins to fall in love.

Tolstoy's epiphanies feel true because they don't create immediate change. Nor do they radically alter a person's identity. They simply put the person in touch with something that was already there. More important, the person might change again in a few weeks, and the revelation will be lost.

Tolstoy works with surprising speed, doing in a sentence or two what many novelists need whole paragraphs to achieve. He also leaps nimbly from one point of view to another. Again and again, we see an emotion inside a character and then how it appears to others. His quickness enables him to show people changing from one week to the next and back again, not in big, permanent strokes but in little jumps, like a jittery time-lapse film of a growing plant. There's a constant buzz of evolution, a blur of change that leaves the characters vulnerable—or adaptable—to major shifts in the environment. A death in the family or the outbreak of war can freeze the last change for the time being.

It's interesting to compare Tolstoy's pace with the pace of *Les Misérables* by Victor Hugo, written a few years earlier (1862) and almost as long. Hugo piles on digressions and sermons and irrelevant history. He throws in seventeen chapters about the Battle of Waterloo to no clear purpose. Many readers give up on the book and turn to one of the many movies made from it or even the musical to find out what happens.

Tolstoy works so quickly and with such exuberance that we don't have time to question his purpose. Look at the wolf hunt with the Rostov family. They and their neighbors and two hundred dogs pursue a she-wolf and her mate, Tolstoy leaping from body to body, rapidly identifying not only the humans but some of the dogs and horses. He even puts us in the skin of the wolves. ("'No difference, I'm going on!' the wolf seemed to say to herself, and she pressed on without looking round.") The episode is not necessary for the story—it's gratuitous, a gift—yet if we think about it later, we realize how much it adds to our picture of Natasha. She takes such pleasure in the hunt. Combined with the next scene, when she performs a folk dance for her peasant "uncle," the hunt puts us solidly on the side of this impulsive, energetic young girl. She will need our sympathy a few chapters later, when she ruins her reputation and destroys her engagement to Andrey by falling in love with a worthless young rake.

Much of the book's dynamic comes from the juxtaposition of civilian life and military life. These are two very different worlds—cozy homes with mothers and sisters, and the rugged, all-male army in foreign places. The two worlds remain apart yet inform and echo each other. (This has special resonance for someone like myself, who grew up in a navy town during the Vietnam War and was surrounded by military families. It all feels so familiar.) Adding to the book's size is the fact that Tolstoy gives both worlds equal attention. He doesn't skimp on the military side, even though one campaign is very much like another and battle scenes can become repetitious.

Tolstoy carefully orchestrates the combat so that the reader doesn't suffer battle fatigue. He begins small, in the Austerlitz campaign, with the skirmish at Enns Bridge, over the Danube. He expands to the rear-guard action at Schoengrabern, where a battery commanded by Captain Tushin covers for the retreating Russian army—Andrey defends Tushin afterward when he's unjustly criticized and comes away feeling that war was nothing like he imagined. The novel builds to a full-scale account of the Battle of Austerlitz seen primarily from the points of view of Nikolay and Andrey, an elaborate sequence that ends with Andrey leading a charge against the French.

The second half of the novel features the Battle of Borodino, and one fears Tolstoy has nothing new to show us. But he adds a new color by presenting this battle from the point of view of a civilian, Pierre, who comes out from Moscow to witness history. He joins the officers on a hilltop—they are happy to show this important civilian around—and looks down into a misty valley full of soldiers and firing cannon. "And the whole scene was writhing, or it looked as if it was, because of the mist and smoke drifting across the entire landscape." Ironically, the civilian will see more of the battle than his friend Andrey, who is wounded when a shell explodes at his feet while he waits with his regiment in the rear.

In each battle, Tolstoy creates an orderly disorder: we get a clear sense of the battlefield as a whole even as we experience the confusion of the individual participants. He deftly mixes the big and the little, close-ups and long shots, almost always from a particular person's point of view. He humanizes battle, replacing distant spectacle with personal drama. And he includes startling shifts of mood and surprising juxtapositions. Nikolay, in his first battle, is shocked to find Frenchmen shooting at him. "They can't be after me! Why? They can't want to kill me! *Me.* Everybody loves me!" Later, at Austerlitz, Andrey is wounded and lies on the ground, flat on his back. Suddenly, in the middle of so much noise and violence, there is silence.

> Above him was nothing, nothing but the sky—the lofty sky, not a clear sky, but infinitely lofty, with grey clouds sweeping gently across. "It's so quiet, peaceful and solemn, not like me rushing about," thought Prince Andrey, "not like us, all that yelling and scrapping . . . those clouds are different, creeping across

that lofty, infinite sky. How can it be that I've never
seen that lofty sky before? Oh, how happy I am to
have found it at last. Yes! It's all vanity, it's all an illusion, everything except that infinite sky."

The surprising notes are sometimes comic and sometimes profound, but all add to the shifting, vibrating
reality of the novel.

Tolstoy's pace and drama and command of details sweep
us backward in time with amazing ease. I think he surprised himself with how much he knew and how real
he could make this experience, more real than anything
he'd written before. For the first half of the book, that
was enough. Not until the second half, after Napoleon
invades Russia, did Tolstoy stop being satisfied with just
telling a story and want to dig around in the meaning
and philosophy of history. I will wait until the final chapter of this book, about epilogues and endings, to discuss
those ideas, but let me say here that I believe the real
meat of *War and Peace* is in its storytelling, not in the
sixty or so pages of woolly commentary—the fifty pages
of the second epilogue and ten pages of passages scattered earlier—that many critics love to discuss.

But one piece of story that shifts *War and Peace*
from the realm of the novel and closer to a work of history is the presence of Napoleon. In most historical

fiction, capital-*h* History—that impersonal force of politics and power—is something that happens completely outside the control of the characters, like the weather. The presence of Napoleon changes that—or should. Napoleon is the demiurge of the novel, its haunting spirit. He is mentioned in the very first sentence. Pierre and Andrey begin by admiring him. (Gore Vidal's Aaron Burr admired him, too.) He appears briefly in person three hundred pages in, when he stands over the wounded Andrey on the battlefield of Austerlitz. Nikolay glimpses him from a distance at his meeting with Tsar Alexander.

We don't see him up close until the start of the second half of the novel, when Tolstoy shows Napoleon at his headquarters, receiving a Russian emissary. He is neither liberator nor Antichrist but a "tubby, dumpy," cranky figure who is not embarrassed to lose his temper in public. In a single scene, Tolstoy knocks to pieces the Great Man theory of history. Nothing in the pages that follow changes that first impression. He remains a mindless nullity, a mysterious puppet. Napoleon only rides the horse of history, thinking he is in control even as the horse takes him wherever it pleases.

Napoleon becomes part of what might be called the zen of Tolstoy: Nothing is what it seems. Nothing goes according to plan, but ordinary people sometimes get what they want. Life is smarter than you are.

The Macro and the Micro

Stories can be told quickly or slowly, frantically or smoothly. There is tempo for narrative, just as there is for music. There are no strict rules, and the range of options is exciting. This is true for both fiction and nonfiction.

One can race through a historical event or prolong it. George R. Stewart draws out a few hours at the Battle of Gettysburg in *Pickett's Charge* much as Proust drew out Albertine's first kiss of the Narrator. It's the Proust trick of riding your bicycle as slowly as possible without falling over. Other writers hurry through an event in order to show it more clearly, in much the same way as actors who are encouraged to speak a speech more quickly so they don't get lost in the tangles.

Stories can also be long or short, macro or micro. Novels tend to work in shorter time periods, while history frequently goes for the long stretch. But the two sometimes switch roles. The material must find its own shape. Tolstoy found his tempo and length while writing *War and Peace*. Earlier I talked about the illusion of real life in real time. Let's call it novel time. This can range from the realistic time of plays and movies to the quick-step narratives of popular history or exposition in fiction. *War and Peace* uses novel time throughout despite Tolstoy's decision to carry his story to 1812. He could not have written a shorter book in the tempo he chose and still span the years and events he wanted to cover.

The writer also needs to discover how much detail a particular story needs to work. Too many details and we can't see the forest for the trees. Too few and we're wandering on the barren plains of generalization. But there are no clear-cut rules about the balance of detail and story. The writer learns it through trial and error.

An interesting example of a work finding its shape is Thomas Babington Macaulay's *History of England.* Nobody reads this once-famous title anymore. It might be the longest, most obscure book I've ever read for pleasure, and I've read some mighty obscure books. I picked up the four-volume set in a secondhand bookstore, and it sat on my shelves unread for decades, until I needed to make room for more books. I thought I should read a chapter or two before I got rid of it. I ended up wolfing down all four volumes.

The first chapters are written in long view, an account of English history from ancient times to the reign of Charles II, dry and elegant but not terribly involving. Then comes the famous social-history chapter, "England in 1685," which is all details, wonderful details: life in London, life in the provinces, the rise of the coffeehouse, the prevalence of highwaymen, the poor education of upper-class women. With the death of Charles II, the book shifts into the kind of dramatic storytelling we associate with novels and even movies. We get scenes and characters and plots—literal plots in this case, intrigue and conspiracy. The book fully comes to life. Macaulay has found the right mix of story and details and tempo, his own personal novel time. He originally intended to cover all of English history up to the reign of George III, but once he fell into this new rhythm, he saw it would be impossible. He kept cutting the story off sooner as he wrote, until he decided to end it with the death of William III. It covers only sixteen years.

What the narrative loses in thematic development it gains in storytelling brio. The book was a remarkable best seller in Britain when it appeared, competing with Dickens. Historians claim it succeeded as patriotic propaganda, but I find that hard to believe when most of the characters are rogues and rotters and the only hero, William III, is a Dutchman. No, the book succeeded as a collection of ripping yarns, with a perfect villain in James II. We are back in the dog-eat-dog world of *Game of Thrones,* only this time with periwigs and muskets and much better manners.

While fiction strives for the condition of history,

many history books hope to achieve the high drama of novels.

Large-scale narrative history was very popular in the nineteenth century, and we can still get pleasure from some of those multivolume sagas. People continue to read Francis Parkman's *France and England in North America,* and understandably so. It's a great read. Like Macaulay, Parkman tells yarns, but his are about the French and English and Hurons and Iroquois in the wilderness. These yarns are woven into the geography, so that the Great Lakes, rivers, and forests become major characters in the book. Parkman is full of prejudices, and they spill into his prose, but his stories frequently contradict his adjectives. Parkman despises the Catholic Church as only a New England Protestant could ("This mighty Church of Rome . . . now a virgin, now a harlot; an imperial queen, and a tinseled actress"), but he can't help admiring the Jesuit missionaries who traveled deep into the interior by canoe and foot to live with Native American tribes and learn their languages. He regularly refers to Indians as "treacherous" or "primitive" or "barbaric," but he often takes their side. He is frustrated they didn't stop fighting each other and band together to drive out the French and English.

His seven volumes succeed because they work as discrete chunks of story, like stepping stones through two and a half centuries. The volume about the Jesuits is followed by one on La Salle and one about Count Frontenac. The English don't even appear until the sixth volume. Unlike Macaulay, he completed what he first conceived, and this mammoth work has a grandeur and a satisfying narrative shape. When the French are defeated in the final volume, *Montcalm and Wolfe*, there's a genuine feeling of conclusion and loss.

Modern historians try to replicate this kind of story-telling but usually end up producing textbooks full of data and dates and dry generalizations. A wonderful exception is *Ecstatic Nation* by Brenda Wineapple, a narrative history of the United States from 1848 to 1877. A biographer as well as a historian, Wineapple scatters three dozen or more pocket portraits of Americans, some famous, some forgotten, throughout the book: John Quincy Adams, Abraham Lincoln, the Fox sisters, Brigham Young, Frederick Douglass, Victoria Woodhull, Jefferson Davis, Dorothea Dix, Robert Smalls, Lydia Maria Child, Andrew Johnson, Clarence King, George Armstrong Custer, and Carl Schurz, to name just a few. This is character-driven history, and one cannot help thinking of Edmund Wilson's description of the people in *Uncle Tom's Cabin:* "They come before us arguing and struggling, like real people who cannot be quiet . . . a flock of lamenting and ranting, prattling and preaching characters, in a drama that demands to be played to the end."

The book is written with great style and verbal energy. Wineapple writes glorious prose:

> After his death it was said that Phineas Taylor Barnum was more alive than anyone still living. Gray-eyed, affable, and six foot two, his jowls a little flabby, he had been funny, extroverted, and aphoristic. And as a producer and prolific writer (though he himself was his best and truest subject), Barnum had represented America to Americans, or so he had hoped. In that way, he was oddly like his contemporary, the controversial poet Walt Whitman; in fact he was the Whitman of the stage: cocky, optimistic, self-centered, a purveyor of the American scene and in a way its singer . . . Barnum loved his audience. In fact, he didn't say there was a sucker born every minute, though the phrase has been attributed to him. Rather, his hodgepodge of curiosities was a kind of democracy in action, embracing everybody and everything.

Wineapple expertly juggles people, facts, and new ideas. But she isn't just telling a familiar story in a fancy voice. She includes the established story lines about the coming of the Civil War and then adds others that are usually left out, such as the democracy of Barnum and Whitman and the separatism of the Mormons in Utah. The Mormons do double duty here, not only evoking the religious spirit of the age but putting a new spin on the issues of popular sovereignty and secession. Wineapple works in long, melodic lines that carry the reader into the war and through the war to the ugly years afterward. The book has no big new revelation, no paradigm-changing gimmick, but it's full of little revelations and fresh discoveries, new connections achieved through solid storytelling.

This kind of large-scale narrative can now be found in other media. The PBS-style documentary pioneered by Ken Burns is a new genre, like an illustrated book with voices. In his lengthy films about baseball or jazz, Burns can get lost in the details, but his brother, Ric Burns, produced a perfect epic in *New York: A Documentary Film*. This is sixteen hours of great TV, constructed out of talking-head shots, old photographs, old movie footage, music, and voice-over narration. Burns knows he cannot say everything about the four-hundred-year history of a city, not even in sixteen hours. So he chooses three dozen or so diverse, articulate characters and a few keys themes and weaves them together to lay down a single trail through a mountain of material. He moves quickly through some events, skips over others, and then lingers over a linchpin episode like the Triangle Shirtwaist fire. An actor reads the words of a newspaper reporter who watched from the street as one girl after another jumped from the burning building to the street below. The scene uses nothing but a voice, music, and a few photos, and it is heartbreaking. Yet the story doesn't stop there. It introduces us to the triumph of the labor movement in New York, which leads to the rise of new ideas about public welfare, ideas that will inform the New Deal, twenty years later. That's just one span in a narrative architecture full of arches and bridges, carrying us from decade to decade.

(My partner is a documentary filmmaker. We both love movies—I love movies as much as I love history—and it was always one of our great bonds. But watching Draper assemble a movie out of bits and pieces of film has made me aware of how similar writing and film editing are. Both are about choices, emphasis, structure, and flow. One shot must lead to the next even as sentence leads to sentence. Writers get to "make up" their pieces of film, but those pieces aren't always as good as the real thing. Draper makes up nothing, and he has no agenda except to tell an interesting story. Much interpretation goes into editing a movie. Draper doesn't think of it as interpretation, however, but as simply making sense of a lot of raw material.)

Large narratives give us the strange pleasure of concentrated time, the satisfaction of viewing a broad vista of years from a single spot. Time becomes less overwhelming when we can experience twenty to fifty to a few hundred years covered in one story.

Fiction can do big pictures, too, but it's rarer and more difficult. By their nature, novels tend to keep inside the space of a single life span. But novelists can't help wanting to break through that constriction.

Orlando by Virginia Woolf uses fantasy to escape the limitations, imagining a man who lives for four hundred years and turns into a woman along the way. Enemies of the book dismiss it as a self-indulgent love letter to Vita Sackville-West, but it's actually a self-indulgent love letter to English literature. Woolf knows her history through literature: from the Elizabethans to the eighteenth century to the Victorian era to the moderns. The chief event in the book is the writing of a single poem, which takes Orlando several centuries.

Woolf has great fun with the stock images people use to characterize past ages. Tudor England is the frail hand of old Queen Elizabeth, a sickly hand curled as if around an orb and attached to a body that smells of camphor; the Victorian age is represented first by bad weather and then by a row of identical town houses, each with a butler at its door and a parrot in the window. Woolf also has enormous fun with the mysteries of history and biography. Frustrated by her inability to pin Orlando down, she concludes toward the end of the book:

> For she had a great variety of selves to call upon, far more than we have been able to find room for, since a biography is considered complete if it merely accounts for six or seven selves, whereas a person may well have as many thousand.

Orlando is a game, a stunt, a high-velocity time machine. Gender disappears in its blur of years, and so does death. It's the only Woolf novel in which nobody dies.

Mr. Mani, by the Israeli novelist A. B. Yehoshua, is a series of dialogues that work backward in time from 1982 to 1848, leaping from period to period as if in a game of hopscotch. Each dialogue begins and ends with biographies of the two participants. We get only one side of the conversation, so they're like interrupted monologues.

> —No. That old coat was given me by his father. Mr. Mani.
> —That's how I think of him. *Mr. Mani.* Don't ask me why.
> —But that's the whole point of my story. That's the only reason I came home today, because it's crazy to be sitting here with you when I should be in Tel Aviv studying for an exam . . .

There are no stage directions. It might sound too clever for its own good, abstract and off-putting, but every dialogue is clear and involving. We even get a strong sense of the silent partner. Each conversation is a story about the Mani family, but only the last speaker is a Mani. They take us step-by-step down into the past and closer to the mystery of the family.

Yehoshua is a remarkable novelist, able to will himself into the skin of almost any person imaginable: male, female, young, old, Jew, Arab, gentile, straight, or gay. He can do it across time as well, both in this novel and one set in the early Middle Ages. *Mr. Mani* begins with a young Israeli woman talking to her mother at a kibbutz but moves on to a Nazi officer in Crete talking to his visiting grandmother; a British lieutenant in Jerusalem during the First World War talking to his superior officer; a young Jewish doctor telling his father in Cracow about the Third Zionist Congress in Switzerland, in 1899; and finally Avraham Mani's conversation with a rabbi debilitated by a stroke, and the rabbi's wife, in Athens in 1848.

Conversation runs like a thread through the different ages. We go from the natural, informal, flippant speech of a modern college student to the elaborate courtesies of an old Sephardic merchant that would not sound out of place in the seventeenth century. I'm sure something is lost in the translation from Hebrew to English, but we are already translating from one era to another. Something is lost, but something is also gained.

The novel is as much about the people who encounter the Manis as it is about the Manis themselves. All are sunnier and more hopeful than this chain of unhappy men. A strain of melancholy and sorrow runs through the Mani family like a curse. It's not the trauma of the Holocaust or the pain of exile that we initially expect. Only at the end do we learn about the sin at the heart of their sorrow, and it's as primal as Greek myth or the Old Testament.

The other end of the scale, the micro, can be just as challenging and exciting. "Small subjects sometimes make good books," writes French historian Emmanuel Le Roy Ladurie in *Montaillou*, his history of a medieval French village. Novelists have long known this, or known that a small piece of a big subject can suggest the whole. *The Leopard* is a smart collection of small pieces. And some novelists go much smaller. *The Death of Virgil* by Hermann Broch covers the last eighteen to thirty-six hours in the life of the Roman poet after his return from Greece. The four-hundred-page novel is all interior monologue except for a hundred-page dialogue with Augustus Caesar. (I confess that I've not been able to do more than pick and nibble at this difficult book. It's not a good sign that no critic knows for certain exactly how many hours pass before Virgil dies.)

Historians play at this end of the scale, too. A fascinating example is *Five Days in London, May 1940* by John Lukacs, not least because it continues his two previous books, *The Last European War*, about the first two years of World War II, and *The Duel*, about the eighty days when Britain decided to continue alone the war against Hitler. We can follow the evolution in storytelling as Lukacs works tighter and tighter, looking for the smallest possible turning point.

War lends itself to microhistory, in both fiction and nonfiction. *The Killer Angels* by Michael Shaara is the Pulitzer Prize–winning novel about the three days of the Battle of Gettysburg. This very popular book is all battle scenes, which is a challenge for any writer, including Tolstoy. Gettysburg is one of the most written-about battles in world history, second only to Waterloo. There are far more such books now than when Shaara published his novel, in 1974. Maybe I've just read too many nonfiction accounts, but his novel makes me feel that fiction might not be the best way to tell this story.

One problem is that the characters are little more than points of view with a few personality quirks. Even Robert E. Lee, a major protagonist, is seen here as just a dyspeptic sad sack who grumbles a lot. The prose includes a tame stream of consciousness of sentence fragments and awkward metaphors:

Lee rested against the rail fence. Cannot depend on Ewell. Nor on Hill. There is only Longstreet. Pickett is fresh. Longstreet has fresh men. Virginians. For whom we broke the vow. Lee shook his head. Well, one thing is sure, if we attack tomorrow, it will be with Longstreet. He meditated a moment, weariness flowing through him like a bleak slow wind. Think *now*, before you get too tired.

There are none of the surprising, striking details that historical writing needs to cut through the clichés and preconceptions. The reader must do most of the work of imagining what's happening, which means the book leaves the battle much as you've already pictured it. This might be why the book is so popular.

I've never read a novel with so many maps, but I'm glad they're there, or I wouldn't know what was going on. This is war as imagined by someone who's played a lot of board games. The good dialogue is out of a John Ford western, but there's much bad expository dialogue in which officers say improbable things to let us know how many men the other side has or who's in command or how many miles away they are. Each side knows far too much about what the other side is doing. The fog of war is missing. But Shaara is religiously committed to "Show, don't tell," and he has no other way to give important information.

My own favorite book about Gettysburg is an earlier work, *Pickett's Charge* by George R. Stewart. Stewart also wrote novels, but he's most famous for his inventive history: *Ordeal by Hunger,* his account of the Donner Party, and *Names on the Land,* an exhilarating dictionary of the United States that uses place-names to capture the wildly pluralistic nature of its people. *Pickett's Charge* is subtitled *A Microhistory of the Final Attack at Gettysburg, July 3, 1863,* and it handles just one event from one day of the brutal three-day battle.

Modern military actions—and the American Civil War was modern—produce an avalanche of information. There are the official records of companies, regiments, brigades, divisions, and corps. Then individuals write up their experiences in letters, diaries, and memoirs. A famous event like Pickett's Charge multiplies the amount of paper tenfold. It's not difficult to find the material for a whole book about this action. What's difficult is to find a way to make the account coherent and interesting. In both fiction and nonfiction, writing well means knowing what to leave out. Military history requires you to throw out truckloads of material, but Stewart makes the bold decision to keep as much as possible.

Despite all the data, however, there are still enormous gaps. Stewart the historian uses as much imagination to get into Lee's thoughts as Shaara the novelist does. After he describes Lee physically ("fifty-six years old, gray-bearded," etc.), he admits:

> Thus we may easily catalogue the exterior. But to tell what he really was—that can tax all men's ingenuity. Some bits of morning mist, they tell us, still hung about the battlefield, and if a little of that mist swirled about him, half-concealing, we may take that as a symbol; for even yet the man, whatever he was, is blurred by the shifting mists of his legend . . .
>
> For our purposes here, however, we need not consider the whole man. We have but one question to ask, "Why did Lee order Pickett's Charge?"

Stewart does not restrict himself to "Show, don't tell" but feels free to narrate, guess, second-guess, analyze. He is able to say things in his own voice that would not sound convincing if stuck in the mouth of a fictional soldier or officer. He is not afraid to use humor. He takes his time telling the story. Earlier I compared his method to the game of riding your bicycle as slowly as possible without falling over. Stewart falls over a few times—not even he can keep the reader interested in a long catalog of Union regiments. But the book ultimately succeeds. It's a remarkable experiment in how much past you can recapture, how "real" you can make a single event. It is full of fascinating details, ranging from the problem of the exact time (watches were un-trustworthy and could not be synchronized) to what it was like for the men of both sides to wait in the hot sun all day (the attack did not take place until after three o'clock) to the inevitable question about toilet facilities:

> As to what were the sanitary arrangements, no one
> has left even a hint—whether because of mid-century
> reticence in such matters, or because of a supposition
> that everyone would know the way such things were
> arranged. Yet we can only think that already a fecal
> odor was mingling with that of dead horses.

By the time we come to the attack itself, over halfway through the book, we have spent more hours in the broken shoes of a Civil War soldier than might be thought possible. But, as Stewart says, "Much of human nature is to be learned on a battlefield."

Pickett's Charge was not so much a charge as a steady march across an open field against the Union position on Cemetery Ridge. As anyone who's visited Gettysburg knows, Cemetery Ridge is not really a ridge but only a slight rise of ground, a tilt of land that makes the open field even more open. After an hour and a half of artillery bombardment, two Confederate divisions (one of them commanded by George Pickett) advanced across the field with flags flying, marching without drums or music. It took them twenty minutes to reach their goal. When the Union opened fire with rifles and cannons—the cannons fired canister, which works like mammoth shotgun blasts—a brigade on the left broke and ran. The rest of the force continued and struck the Union lines hard. Men fired at each other at close range for thirty endless minutes. There was almost no hand-to-hand fighting. The rebel yell was heard only once, during the rush of a stone wall known as the Angle. The Union regiments didn't break. Finally the Confederates began to give way, first on the flanks and then in the center. The withdrawal turned into a retreat, with soldiers scattering across the field.

Miraculously, Stewart is able to make this frantic hour clear and coherent. He breaks the action into numbered sections, some long, some as short as a paragraph, like scenes in a screenplay. They flow together like rushing water.

Pickett's Charge is also the climax of *The Killer Angels*. Shaara presents it solely from the point of view of one man, Brigadier General Lewis Armistead, who appears late in the novel. We walk with him and his brigade from their muster area into the open field and up the slight slope to the Union lines and death. It's the high point of the book, a powerful scene full of color and immediacy, but it's more spectacle than drama, showing us courage but without exploring its human nature.

The Confederate dead and wounded totaled almost 6,000, more than half the 10,000 men who participated in the assault. The Union losses totaled only 1,500. The assault became known as the high-water mark of the Confederacy. We don't know if success would have produced victory or if victory would have won the war for the South—Lee needed not just another win but a total disaster for the North. Another year and nine months of war loomed ahead. But after the war the myth arose that if Pickett had succeeded, the South could have won.

Stewart never quotes the most famous passage about Pickett's Charge, William Faulkner's romantic rhapsody in *Intruder in the Dust:* "For every Southern boy fourteen years old, not once but whenever he wants it, there is the instant when it's still not yet two oclock on that July afternoon in 1863, the brigades are in position behind the rail fence, the guns are laid and ready in the woods and the furled flags are already loosened to break out and Pickett himself with his long oiled ringlets and his hat in one hand probably and his sword in the other looking up the hill waiting for Longstreet to give the word and it's all in the balance, it hasn't happened yet, it hasn't even begun yet . . ."

This was true only for Faulkner's generation, of course, and maybe the next. But even then one can't help wanting to correct the opening phrase: "For every Southern *white* boy . . ."

Exhibit D: American Slavery

The 2014 Golden Globe Awards were hosted by comedians Tina Fey and Amy Poehler, two smart women with a gift for knocking conventional wisdom on its ear with a simple, well-placed sentence. When they came to the difficult, often brutal, highly praised movie *12 Years a Slave,* Poehler blithely declared, "I can honestly say I will never look at slavery the same way again." Fey gave her a shocked double take. "Wait," said Fey, "how were you looking at it before?"

It was a joke, of course, but a joke that cut in different directions. On one level it said that slavery was so terrible, only a fool would believe there was more than one way to look at it. On another level, the joke mocked the movie, claiming it told us nothing new: we already know slavery was terrible. But where does that leave us? Does that mean we don't have to think about slavery at all? How do we think about the unthinkable?

History can be an escape, an entertainment. But we also believe that history is good for us, providing perspective and hard knowledge. And no knowledge is harder than American slavery. A mix of history books and novels should enable us to see any historical subject more clearly, even the impossible subject of slavery.

When I grew up in Virginia, in the early 1960s, our seventh-grade history book, *Virginia: History, Government, Geography*, presented slavery as a problematic yet benign institution. Oh, it was wrong, of course, and an occasional bad master could be cruel and abusive, but most slaves were treated kindly. Over the next decade, however, that sentimental myth was replaced by the angry, harsher picture of slavery as something like the concentration camps of the Nazis, a nightmare of unspeakable horror. It became so horrible that people didn't want to hear about it at all. Many moviegoers couldn't bring themselves to see *12 Years a Slave*, despite the rave reviews. But while most reviewers claimed that the movie had finally given us a true picture of slavery, one reviewer, a black man, dismissed the film as "torture porn."

How do we write about slavery without seeming to apologize for it or treating it as the stuff of sadomasochist pornography? We can begin by remembering that slavery was a "human" institution. That's a peculiar word for this soul-killing crime. Yet it was something that otherwise good men and women and their children did to other men, women, and children.

"Cruel, unjust, exploitative, oppressive," declares historian Eugene D. Genovese on the first page of *Roll, Jordan, Roll*, "slavery bound two peoples together in a bitter antagonism while creating an organic relationship so complex and ambivalent that neither could express the simplest human feelings without reference to the other." It's a powerful summation. But what was the experience like? How did it feel to be owned? Or to be the owner?

We see the general outline in good social history like *Roll, Jordan, Roll* or *The Peculiar Institution* by Kenneth M. Stampp or the powerful first chapters of *Black Reconstruction in America* by W. E. B. DuBois. Now and then an anecdote or story catches the reader's imagination and brings the experience to life. But the experience disappears back into the general facts and figures that are necessary to scholarly history. The DuBois, Stampp, and Genovese books aren't volumes to read cover to cover but to roam in, like encyclopedias. There's no narrative to hold them together. Narrative makes an experience more human, whether it's fiction or nonfiction.

We don't get close to slavery or begin to feel it until we read a personal story. Some of the classic slave narratives are good for this, such as *Incidents in the Life of a Slave Girl,* but many are too thick with rhetoric to speak directly to us. Even the great Frederick Douglass is stronger on moral ideas than he is on firsthand experience. We must go to fiction to get the rest of the story. The most popular and influential book about slavery,

Roots by Alex Haley, is a curious hybrid that begins as a novel (the life of Kunta Kinte, the African, is mostly imagined), then becomes novelized history, then history, and ends as memoir.

There is a strong element of fiction in many of the first-person narratives about slavery, both the good and the bad ones. *Narrative of William W. Brown* was written by William Wells Brown, a fugitive slave who went on to write novels *(Clotel; or, The President's Daughter)* as well as history. Some of the slave narratives were cowritten by or written for abolitionists who wanted to emphasize the institution's horror, and the easiest way to do this was to feature the whip. (Brown introduces a whip "with platted wire" on the very first page.) Historians are still sorting out fact from fiction in *Twelve Years a Slave* by Solomon Northup, the book that became the movie.

But how important is literal factuality if a book makes an experience real for us? Let's go back to Harriet Jacobs's *Incidents in the Life of a Slave Girl.* As I said earlier, the book was once believed to be a novel. It makes an interesting counterexample to Mary Chestnut's *Diary from Dixie,* the detailed, observant record of the well-read wife of a member of the Confederate administration. The diary was used for years as a primary source by historians until C. Vann Woodward discovered that Chestnut had revised and expanded her actual diary to create a novel in diary form. She died before she could publish it. Historians now avoid it, although the book offers as much insight as fiction as it did when it was nonfiction.

Jacobs's memoir has the ring of—if not truth, then of messy reality, whether it's fiction or nonfiction. It is a truly strange story, this tale of a pretty girl pursued by her master and hiding in an attic like Anne Frank. It's hardly a universal slave experience, but the best stories are never generic. The strengths of *Incidents* become clearer once we know the real names and places that correspond to Jacobs's pseudonyms. Jean Yellin's biography anchors Jacobs's personal experience in social and historical reality. We see that the worlds of white and black, free and slave, were more mixed than we imagine. The free grandmother is a remarkable character who lives in two worlds, a salamander able to endure both fire and ice. The story also reminds us that slave owners could not do anything they wanted to their human property. There were legal and social as well as psychological limits. White people cared what the neighbors thought. Yet Jacobs includes her own tales of horror, which are more startling in the context of a recognizably human world. (The most horrific is that of a runaway slave being locked for four days and nights in a boxlike cotton gin as punishment. He is found dead one morning, his corpse half-eaten by rats.)

Jacobs's plain prose adds force to her story. White contemporaries thought it showed her lack of education, but modern readers often find it sharper and more engaging than the prose of Frederick Douglass. She grabs our attention with her first sentence: "I was born a slave; but I never knew it till six years of happy childhood had passed away." When she is only fifteen, her master, Dr. Flint, presses her to be his mistress, whispering "foul words in my ear." Mrs. Flint jealously hates the girl. Her free grandmother works to keep the peace. But then Harriet is courted by a single white man, Mr. Sands, and becomes pregnant by him. Dr. Flint attends the birth (he's the only doctor in town), sees the baby is half-white, and is furious. He bars her from his home, where the child is raised—as his property. Then Harriet has a second child by Mr. Sands.

Harriet cannot flee north, for fear of getting caught and because she can't leave her two children. When Dr. Flint threatens to sell her south, her grandmother and uncle build a hiding place under the eaves of the grandmother's house, a nine-foot-long cell. Harriet drills a small hole and can see out to the street, watching the passage of her children below. She stays here for seven years! No wonder so many historians thought the book must be a novel. She helplessly watches the life of the town like a ghost in the eaves.

Mr. Sands buys his children from Dr. Flint. He marries a white woman and confesses that the boy and girl are his son and daughter. Mrs. Flint gloats when the little boy is attacked by a dog, hoping that his mother hears about it and it will break her heart. The Flints believe Harriet has fled north, never dreaming she is living just above their heads. Small-town lives, white and black, slave and free, are tangled and ingrown in ways now hard to imagine. Again, truth is stranger than fiction.

The grandmother and uncle finally arrange secret passage on a sailing ship for Harriet. On the trip north, she sits on deck and enjoys the sun and wind for the first time in years.

William Styron begins with nonfiction in his controversial 1967 novel *The Confessions of Nat Turner.* Turner led a slave revolt in Virginia in 1831. He and his followers killed roughly sixty men, women, and children before the revolt was crushed. After he was caught, Turner dictated a confession, which was published as a pamphlet. Styron expands on the confession in a bold, dangerous book that still has its enemies.

The actual historical confession, which is less than twenty pages, reads like legal boilerplate.

Sir,—You have asked me to give a history of the motives which induced me to undertake the late

insurrection, as you call it—To do so I must go back
to the days of my infancy, and even before I was born.
I was thirty-one years of age the 2d of October last,
and born the property of Benj. Turner, of this county.

Styron gives Nat a different voice, an invented prose
style that suggests a disciplined Faulkner, the lush, long,
run-on sentences given stronger shape and more precise content. Styron can get carried away with his descriptions, but that's actually a benefit in a historical
novel. We are happy to see a lost world made visible,
whether it's in the extended account of an abandoned
plantation, or the torchlit glimpse of a pocket watch,
blue hair ribbon, and quill pen on a night table in the
middle of the killing, or the memory of a slave cemetery.

My grandmother died within days of my mother's
birth, refusing to eat, falling into a stupor until the
moment of her last breath, when it was said that the
black skin turned to the gray of ashes, collapsing in
upon the inhabiting bones until the body of the child
(for that is what she was) seemed so fragile as to be
almost weightless, like a whitened, burnt-out stick
of lightwood ready to crumble at the softest touch.
For years there was a cedar headboard in the Negro
graveyard, not far from the mill, with carved letters
which read:

"Tig"
AET. 13
BORN AN
HEATHEN
DIED BAP-
TISED IN CHRIST
A.D. 1782
R.I.P.

When Nat returns a year later, the graveyard has been burned off and the field planted with sweet potatoes.

We quickly accept the prose as an ideal language, not a literal one. The speech of the whites is as awkward and accented as the speech of other blacks, in contrast to this fluent inner voice. Nat is clear, cool, and observant, but underneath his quiet tone is his firm belief that he is a tool of the Lord and must do as he is commanded. He ponders a text by Ezekiel: "Slay utterly old and young, both maids and little children, and women." He seems like the calmest madman imaginable.

The book has a sophisticated flashback structure that provides a solid foundation for the detail-rich prose and leisurely pace. It begins with Nat in his jail cell after his capture. We then jump back to the detailed account of a single day a few years earlier, a day in the life of a slave when nothing too terrible happened, like *One Day in the Life of Ivan Denisovich,* Aleksandr Solzhenitsyn's novel about the prison camps of the gulag, or the chapter "A Good Day" from *Survival in Auschwitz* by Primo Levi. Judge Cobb visits the Travis farm, gets drunk on applejack, and watches in amused disgust as the family punishes a slave, Hark, for misbehavior by forcing him to climb a tree and leaving him stranded and frightened there—Travis forbids whipping, but Hark is terrified of heights. The drunken judge shakes his head. "It is like living in a dream," he grumbles. Slavery has made everyone, white and black, insane. Judge Cobb will preside at Nat's trial for conspiracy and murder.

Next we go back further, to Nat's childhood, a time when his life did not seem so different from that of white children, much like the childhood of Harriet Jacobs. All children are slaves, in effect. Nat's intelligence gets the attention of his master, who has great plans for him: he will apprentice Nat to a carpenter, and Nat will work for wages and eventually buy his freedom. But his master goes broke and loses his plantation and sells off Nat along with the others. Nat's awakening comes when he tells his new master that he's hungry and is struck with a whip for the first time in his life. After pages of hope and dignity, this single blow across the neck is as shocking as murder.

Styron builds Nat's world from outside. He later discussed in an essay the liberties he took with the historical record. The real Nat knew only small farms, but Styron wanted to give a full picture of slavery, so he showed Nat growing up on a large plantation. The novel becomes a panorama of slavery. Historian Martin Duberman wrote that the book might be a flawed novel, but it's impeccable history. There is some question over whether or not Nat had a wife. One is mentioned in the oral tradition but not in the confession or court record. Styron decided to make Nat a celibate in order to increase his religious fervor.

The tension of the novel can take its toll on the reader. We sympathize deeply with Nat when he suffers; we cannot easily detach ourselves when he begins to kill. He and his men murder not just the guilty but also the innocent. A young white woman, Margaret Whitehead, was the only person the real Nat killed himself on his day of wrath. Styron naturally wants this to mean something in the novel, so he imagines a friendship between Nat and Margaret. But the white author has more trouble imagining a good white woman than he does imagining any of his black characters. I believe her pity and Nat's anger, but not Nat's lust. Margaret represents love, a love like charity or forgiveness. Nat's lust only confuses the issue—which might be the point.

Styron's goal was to paint the portrait of a famous black man, but first he needed to re-create slavery for the modern reader. I believe he succeeded in the second goal—this remains the best single evocation of slavery I've ever read—but maybe not in his primary goal. The black critics who attacked the novel a year after it appeared, in *William Styron's Nat Turner: Ten Black Writers Respond,* were furious not only that a white novelist had taken an African American hero as his subject, but also that he had presented him as conflicted and confused. Yet nothing written about Turner since has been as vivid or convincing as Styron's novel.

Toni Morrison in *Beloved* comes to slavery *after* slavery, treating it as an old wound too painful to describe directly. This is a novel about the scar tissue of slavery.

It begins as a ghost story. A small house outside Cincinnati is haunted by an unhappy, angry spirit, the ghost of a two-year-old child. Sethe and her children live with this spirit for eighteen years after their escape from slavery in Kentucky. The spirit moves furniture, leaves tiny handprints in cake, and throws the family dog against a wall. The two sons flee the house. Sethe's mother-in-law, Baby Suggs, dies, and Sethe is left alone with her daughter Denver. It is now 1873. An old friend from slave days, Paul D. Garner, moves in with them. When he and Sethe talk about their plantation days at Sweet Home, Denver scornfully says, "How come everybody run off from Sweet Home can't stop talking about it? Look like if it was so sweet you would have stayed."

This is a novel written almost entirely in extreme close-up, like poetry, and it works. The perspective that felt wrong for a political tale like *Wolf Hall* feels right for a deeply personal story like this one. What can be more personal than the treelike pattern of whip scars on Sethe's back? There is real scar tissue in this novel. What can be more intimate than memories of the death of one's own child? Morrison takes us deep inside her characters' memories and puts us in their skin, making their experience physical, visceral. Slavery has been written on the body.

The book is constructed out of interior monologues, deep solitudes: A man and a woman sharing a bed after sex think their own stories to themselves, a thousand miles apart. A daughter imagines herself inside the story her mother told her of her own birth. Mixing folk tale and fairy tale, the novel often seems timeless, outside history, but then Morrison will drop in a period detail, like a ghost dress with a bustle, and the reader remembers with a jolt that we're in the 1870s.

The new family attends a carnival on Colored Thursday for the privilege of seeing white folks make spectacles of themselves: a fat lady, a giant, a two-headed man. While they are gone, the ghost of the two-year-old child is reborn as Beloved. A full-grown, fully dressed woman of nineteen or twenty rises out of the river and dries herself on the bank, like a butterfly fresh from its chrysalis. She is waiting for them on the porch steps when they come home. They don't know her, but they take her in. She speaks in a low, gravelly voice. Denver looks after her as she would a dog or baby sister. Paul D is skeptical, disliking the hungry, possessive way she looks at Sethe. Denver understands first who Beloved really is. The four protagonists grow more jealous and distrustful of one another. The ghost story continues, in full daylight.

The novel is so famous that it's hard to imagine that people don't know the secret of Beloved's death. It must be as well-known as what happens to Anna Karenina or the truth about Norman Bates's mother in *Psycho*. Yet Morrison withholds it until the second half of the novel and doesn't fully reveal the cruelty that produced the crime until later. (The crime itself actually happened, the act of a runaway slave named Margaret Garner. But Garner died in slavery of typhoid fever and did not see freedom, as Sethe did. Morrison builds a very different story around a grain of historical fact.)

This is a difficult novel, not only in its contents but its form. There are times when the narrative becomes paralyzed by the horror of the story it's telling, and Morrison resorts to soliloquies and even poetry.

She said you wouldn't hurt me.

She hurt me.

I will protect you.

I want her face.

Don't love her too much.

I am loving her too much.

Watch out for her; she can give you dreams.

Beloved succeeds in giving us dreams even as it recovers private lives—personal destinies—from the crushing machinery of slavery.

But what about the other side of the equation? What was it like to own another human being? The idea plays into fantasies of having total power over another person, but the facts are more complicated and more human. In *Landon Carter's Uneasy Kingdom,* a biography by Rhys Isaac, an eighteenth-century planter repeatedly dreams that his runaway slaves have returned to him. He loves what he owns and is hurt when his property doesn't love him back. There's a remarkable chapter in *Roll, Jordan, Roll,* "The Moment of Truth," in which Genovese describes how, during the Civil War, white Southern households serenely believed that their slaves were completely loyal to them. Then came a day when they woke up and found that their "family" had fled. They felt shocked and betrayed, their assumptions about their "people" exposed as lies. (DuBois gives the experience a more revolutionary meaning by calling it "the General Strike.")

As American family life grows looser and kinder, I wonder if we lose the emotional vocabulary necessary for a more complex understanding of slavery. The old-style patriarchal family was held together by force and fear, obedience and shame. Many of the more humane slaveholders sincerely believed their slaves were members of their extended families. All their talk of "our people" and "our family" was not just propaganda but deeply felt delusion. And some of the slaves may have felt it themselves. One of the shocking truths in Quentin Tarantino's revenge fantasy *Django Unchained* is revealed through Samuel L. Jackson's character, a slave who identifies so strongly with his master, he's more dangerous than the whites. It's a fantasy, too, but one that contains a bitter reality. (I like to think Jackson based his character on Supreme Court justice Clarence Thomas.)

When slave owners took the trouble to remember that their property was human, one of their strongest emotions was fear. Alan Taylor explores this in a brilliant book, *The Internal Enemy*, about slavery in Virginia after the American Revolution. Letters and newspapers of the time were full of talk of "the internal enemy," the slaves who might rise up one day and murder the owners and

THE ART OF HISTORY   121

their children. These were the fears of people with guilty consciences; they were not borne out by fact until Nat Turner's revolt decades later. When British warships filled Chesapeake Bay for two years during the War of 1812, the slaves didn't use the opportunity to kill their masters but to escape to the ships and flee to freedom. Taylor is a fine writer, able to tell small stories as well as large ones, mixing tales of money, marriage, and family with the bigger narratives of war and politics. He is also an amazing researcher. Among the most fascinating documents in this fascinating book are the letters written by free men and women in Canada and Trinidad to their former masters. They include proud descriptions of their new lives, requests for news of friends left behind, and even good wishes to the old owners. The whites kept these letters not for sentiment but to pass on to the federal government to prove the loss of their slaves and be reimbursed. So much for the myth of family ties.

Black Masters by Michael P. Johnson and James L. Roark tells a very unexpected story, the history of a free black family in South Carolina who owned slaves. William Ellison of Camden was freed around 1815 by the master who may have also been his father. A skilled carpenter and blacksmith who specialized in building cotton gins, Ellison soon earned enough money to purchase the freedom of his wife and two of his children.

(He later purchased his daughter as well, but could not free her because manumission was outlawed in the state in 1820.) The family at one time owned thirty slaves and two large houses, one of which was named Wisdom Hall.

The book is based on census records, wills, and inventories, with only a few bread-and-butter letters to give voices to the Ellison family. The authors use social history to flesh out the story. In fact, the book succeeds as a work of social history hung upon a few names. The dramatic climax is the enslavement crisis of 1860, when South Carolinians launched a campaign against free blacks. The existence of people like the Ellisons was too confusing in a world where blacks were supposed to be dependent and helpless. A bill was proposed that would legally re-enslave all free blacks still in the state after a certain date. Free blacks began to sell their property and flee, much as Jews fled Germany after Hitler came to power. Only the outbreak of the Civil War ended the campaign. The authors know little about the Ellisons' reaction to the crisis, only that the grandchildren were sent to a school in Philadelphia.

The Ellison saga is a remarkable story in itself, but we can't help wondering what slavery was like in this family without racial difference. If we subtract race from the experience, how did it feel? Was it kinder? Less humiliating? Or did it feel more personal without the gulf of race to "justify" the difference in status? Unfortunately there is nothing in the letters or even interviews with descendants to suggest how the experience changed for either the owner or the owned.

This silence leaves the subject wide open for novelists, and it's surprising more haven't explored it. *The Known World* by Edward P. Jones is famous as a fictional portrait of a black slave owner in Virginia, but it's actually about other things. The novel opens with the 1855 death of Henry Townsend, the black owner of thirty-three slaves, but then slides off into different tales, giving us many, many characters over the course of a century. This is a shattered mirror of a book, a concussion of stories, like a North American *One Hundred Years of Solitude* but even harder to follow. People are barely established before we're hit with a new batch of names. Jones includes much of the population of fictional Manchester County—blacks, whites, slaves, slave owners, free folk, foreigners, runaways, and the local sheriff. Henry is soon forgotten.

The novel clearly works for some readers, but it doesn't for me. Jones is a gifted short-story writer— his collection *Lost in the City* is very fine—but he spreads himself awfully thin here. Henry is presented as a mystery to be solved, but he is dropped unsolved. The book's real focus is how black and white lives are knotted together, bleeding and melting into each other, contrary to the Old South myth of separate worlds. It's a great subject, but there are too many half-sketched characters and unfinished stories and jumps in time for the narrative to fully take hold.

Other novels explore this guilty, tangled knotting in their own ways. *Absalom, Absalom!* by William Faulkner might be the most famous, with its convoluted portrait of Sutpen's Hundred, a raw plantation in the wilderness where whites and blacks prey upon each other. We see it in a gentler form in *Jubilee* by Margaret Walker, which is like *Downton Abbey* set in Georgia among masters and slaves. But the most striking and surprising example is in *Middle Passage* by Charles Johnson.

A free black man, Rutherford Calhoun, narrates the tale of working on a slave ship in the 1830s during the ghastly Middle Passage. What's surprising about the book is that it's a comedy. Calhoun is flippant and smart-ass, a happy thief who flees a shotgun marriage to a woman with a nose "like a doorknob" and stows away on a rotting ship, the *Republic,* bound for the coast of Africa. The captain is Ebenezer Falcon, a dynamic dwarf with "a great bulging forehead that looked harder than whale-bone, but intelligent too—a thinker's brow, it was, the kind fantasy writers put on spacemen far ahead of us in science and philosophy."

This 1990 novel is filled with deliberate anachronisms. There is even a joke about affirmative action. After the solemnity of most slave stories, it's a relief to read a book that thumbs its nose at both realism and gravitas. This is Herman Melville's *Benito Cereno* retold as a Richard Pryor monologue. The jokey language vividly evokes shipboard life (Calhoun wakes up "choking on the rank male sweat that hung around my hammock like wet clothing") even as it plays games with storytelling.

Horror still creeps in, but it's the horror of the slave trade, more vicious than that of any plantation. Calhoun sees forty members of the Allmuseri tribe, men, women, and children, packed into the ship's hold at a port in West Africa.

> It was then that my hair started going white . . .
> I wondered . . . how in God's name I could go on after
> this? How could I feel whole after seeing it? How
> could I tell my children of it without placing a curse
> on them forever? How could I even dare to *have*
> children in a world so senseless?

The Allmuseris are a peaceful people who know magic. Calhoun befriends their leader, Ngonyama, and a little girl, Baleka. Also on board is a large crate containing a mysterious beast. Only the cabin boy gets a glimpse of the creature, and it drives him mad, much as Pip the cabin boy in *Moby-Dick* goes mad after floating for days in the ocean. (Melville haunts this novel.) The Allmuseris rebel and seize the ship. Only Calhoun and three whites survive. Despite the color of his skin, Calhoun is more American than African: we wait to see whose side he will take. What began as comedy turns more dreamlike and disturbing. The ship drifts south, deteriorating as the survivors sicken. The novel ends as a chilling parable about greed that cuts across the color line.

American slavery took place in the "gray zone," Primo Levi's phrase for the moral murk of the Nazi concentration camps. An evil institution takes away everyone's innocence, even that of the victims. Jews became *kapos* if they wanted to live, assisting Nazis in the management of other Jews. Levi refuses to judge his fellow prisoners. Not all camps were death camps, although death was the ultimate end for Jews, Gypsies, Russians, and Poles. I keep coming back to the Nazi camps, since they are one of the few modern analogies we have for slavery. Yet the work camps lasted only 4 years, while American slavery lasted 250. And Africans actually multiplied and endured. Slavery didn't kill off its victims. It was more insidious, more seductive, more like everyday life under capitalism, despite its cruelty and hopelessness. This might be why a Marxist like DuBois can speak of it with less anger than one expects in *Black*

Reconstruction. His chapter on slaves is titled "The Black Worker" and is followed by a chapter titled "The White Worker" Like it or not, we are all in this together.

But in the middle of great suffering, people carved out lives. They made families. They created their own culture. Genovese's book *Roll, Jordan, Roll* is subtitled *The World the Slaves Made.* People were not so dehumanized that they stopped being human, that they no longer had stories to tell. We want to feel nothing but pity and horror when we talk about slavery, but we must also feel more complicated emotions, including respect. Edmund Morgan, in an essay about slavery, "The Big American Crime," quotes a former slave who was interviewed in the 1930s. The man refused to be pitied by his white interviewer. "You know, you still got the disease, honey . . . Talking about giving me this and giving me that right. You talking about giving me something I was born with just like you was born with it. You can't give me the right to be a human being. I was born with that right. Now you can keep me from having that if you've got all the policemen and all the jobs on your side you can deprive me of it, but you can't give it to me, cause I was born with it just like you was."

The Comedy of History

Everybody knows the tragedy of history—we cannot forget it—but we rarely hear about the comedy of history. "He who laughs / Has not yet heard / The terrible news," wrote Bertolt Brecht. Yet there is no denying that the past is often very funny.

The humor can be in the subject itself or in the voice of the author or in a combination of the two. It can be a teaspoon of honey for bitter medicine—which is how Charles Johnson uses it in *Middle Passage.* It can be entertainment, amusement, relief. Best of all, comedy can be a truth teller, a reality test, a bullshit detector.

Probably the most famous work of comic history is *Eminent Victorians* by Lytton Strachey. He was preceded by Edward Gibbon, but the jokes in *Decline and Fall of the Roman Empire* come only every hundred pages or so and can be awfully snarky. ("Of [Pope John] . . . the most scandalous charges were suppressed; the vicar of Christ was only accused of piracy, murder, rape, sodomy, and incest.") Strachey gives us two or three humorous turns of phrase on every page, and they are often direct and friendly. He regularly teases and mocks his subjects—Cardinal Manning, Florence Nightingale, Dr. Thomas

Arnold, and Gordon of Khartoum—but his jokes make his people more human.

The Nightingale portrait is the strongest and most memorable. Strachey opens by declaring that the myth of the Lady with the Lamp visiting the hospitals of Scutari during the Crimean War isn't nearly as interesting as the reality. "A Demon possessed her. Now demons, whatever else they may be, are full of interest. And so it happens that in the real Miss Nightingale there was more that was interesting than in the legendary one; there was also less that was agreeable." He makes fun of her, but most of his comedy is directed at the society that opposed her. His humor becomes scalding when he talks about her enemies. His bitter jokes about the stupidity of the British high command can still move one to indignation. He takes her side when an incompetent medical superior is awarded a knighthood and she wonders if the letters *KCB* stand for "Knight of the Crimean Burial-grounds."

Strachey's account of the heroic period at Scutari, when Nightingale and her volunteers cleaned out the foul, filthy, rat-infested army hospitals and brought in fresh air, clean water, and modern nursing, is masterful. Then he tells the story of the next fifty years, and things become more complicated. Nightingale's demon drove her to battle army bureaucrats to improve soldiers' lives, winning new enemies and wearing out old friends, all from her sickbed—Crimea broke her health—where she wrote endless books and letters. (A later biographer, Cecil Woodham-Smith, includes the wonderful detail that Nightingale's letters were frequently decorated with the inky paw prints of her cats.) Yet she outlived her enemies, her overworked friends, and even her demon. She became gentler in old age. Strachey continues to make jokes to the end, but he clearly misses her old fury.

Eminent Victorians was a best seller during the First World War and was even read in the trenches. A few years ago I tried to teach it to my class in short biography. They were a smart group who could appreciate Oliver Sacks, William Maxwell, and Janet Malcolm, but they were thrown by Strachey, put off by his old-fashioned diction and alien concerns. Almost nobody appreciated his use of comedy to knock down pious righteousness—nobody except an Iranian student, a young woman whose mother had been imprisoned under the mullahs. This student was also a very big Woody Allen fan. She understood hypocrisy, Victorian and Islamic, and knew that scornful laughter was a perfectly valid response.

Many historians learned from Strachey that a writer can make jokes and still be serious. One of the best is Nancy Mitford. A fine comic novelist in her own right

(*Love in a Cold Climate* out-Waughs the upper-class comedy of her friend Evelyn Waugh), Mitford was also a highly entertaining historian who wrote repeatedly about the glamour and absurdity of eighteenth-century court life, chiefly that of Versailles.

Let's look at her wry, witty, worldly biography *Madame de Pompadour.* Born with the plain family name Poisson (Fish), this bourgeois daughter of a tax collector was told by a fortune-teller as a child that she'd be loved by the king, Louis XV. She was obsessed with the king throughout her adolescence, even after she married minor nobility. Then, in 1745, she finally met Louis at the Ball of the Yew Trees, where he was dressed as a large tree. Within a few months she was his mistress. She was twenty-four, Louis thirty-five. He gave her a title, the Marquise de Pompadour, while her husband was awarded a deed of separation and a profitable post in the provinces.

Francis Parkman, in *France and England in North America,* treats her as a cunning Lady Macbeth, but for Mitford she is a heroine: charming, kind, intelligent, and honest. She was friends with many of the philosophes, including Voltaire. I like to think that Mrs. Comstock, my English teacher, knew and loved this book.

The king was still married, but the queen, after giving birth to ten children, had withdrawn into religion and card playing. Pompadour courted her after winning her husband, wanting to be her friend. She even offered to join the queen in her hobby of washing the feet of the poor. This was a strange world, in which the sacred mixed with the profane and adulterers attended mass every morning. Later, when Pompadour briefly found religion herself, she stopped wearing rouge and ordered the secret stairway between her rooms and the king's walled up.

Life in court included cliques and hierarchies, elaborate rituals and Byzantine rules. Choice apartments were fought over like corner offices. There was much insult and gossip, including nasty anonymous poems called Poissonades, about the little bourgeois in their midst. Versailles frequently feels like an even meaner version of high school. But Mitford doesn't make the mistake the Victorians did when they assumed that a life of pleasure was empty and boring. She understands that these people were having a good time.

> The four main pastimes were love, gambling, hunting, and the official entertainments. Love was played like a game, or like a comedy by Marivaux; it had, of course, nothing to do with marriage. Children, in those days, were married off in their teens, and these little husbands and wives usually grew up to be very fond of each other, sharing the same interests,

absorbed in the family and its fortunes. Even if they did not like each other, which was rare, they could generally manage to get on, since good manners demanded that they should.

We are very far from the worlds of *Nat Turner* and *Beloved.*

In time the king and his mistress stopped being lovers and became only intimate friends. The king turned to a private brothel and minor nobility for sex. Pompadour accepted this just as the queen had accepted Pompadour, but it didn't stop the courtiers from gossiping and making jokes about them.

The comedy ended with the Seven Years' War. The court found mirth even here, in the many defeats and the loss of Canada—they found the Lisbon earthquake hysterical. Yet Pompadour was grieved by her country's failure. She advised the king and wrote endless letters of support. She had no real power, but the people blamed her for the victories of England and Prussia. After all, they couldn't blame the king.

She was only forty when she died of pneumonia. The king could not attend her funeral, but he stood on his balcony without a hat or coat, weeping as her funeral cortege left Versailles for Paris.

Death is present even in comic Eden. *Et ego in Arcadia:* "I too am in Arcadia," says Death in many paintings and poems. But death and comedy are not mutually exclusive.

Smart historians use humor in their work, and they use it in different ways. Charles Royster's *The Fabulous History of the Dismal Swamp Company* isn't actually funny, but its digressive style is a history equivalent of the comic run-on voice of a story like Eudora Welty's "Why I Live at the P.O." David McCullough and Brenda Wineapple both use comedy in their books as human notes, breaks in the solemnity, escapes from seriousness. George Stewart and Evan Connell use it, too, but in a dry, bitter manner, often as gallows humor.

There is a reality principle at work here. If one can make a joke about an emotion, and the emotion isn't exposed as silly or fake, then that emotion must be real. Humor also makes action seem more lifelike.

This is true in fiction, too, where comedy is not limited by facts and has freer rein. But writing comic historical fiction requires enormous knowledge, imagination, and confidence. It's like making jokes in a foreign language.

> People do not give it credence that a fourteen-year-old girl could leave home and go off in the wintertime to avenge her father's blood but it did not seem so

strange then, although I will say it did not happen every day. I was just fourteen years of age when a coward going by the name of Tom Chaney shot my father down in Fort Smith, Arkansas, and robbed him of his life and his horse and $150 in cash money plus two California gold pieces that he carried in his trouser band.

True Grit by Charles Portis is a comic gem, a first-person tale told by Mattie Ross about her adventures as a teenager. And it's a wonderful historical novel. Mattie speaks in the deadest of deadpan voices, a Buster Keaton prose that pretends to reveal nothing but is full of feeling. Portis must've read scores of Old West memoirs and dime novels to get the tone exactly right, as well as to capture the slang and wealth of details.

Mattie's narrative is full of surprising digressions, bitter religious beliefs, and harsh revelations. She knows a lot about horses, guns, cooking, bank documents, and bookkeeping. The story itself is very simple, occupying only a couple of weeks in 1875. Determined to find the killer of her father, she goes to Fort Smith and hires a hard-drinking federal marshal named Rooster Cogburn, who looks like a one-eyed Grover Cleveland. ("Some people will say, well there were more men in the country at that time who looked like Cleveland than did not. Still, that is how he looked.") He isn't the laconic hero of Western legend but a real chatterbox, full of endless stories when he's drunk or needs to keep himself awake. They are soon joined by a younger man, a Texas ranger named LaBoeuf, also hunting for Chaney.

Mattie takes her time describing the pursuit into the Oklahoma territory, shifting the story from the realm of movies into real time, a world full of vivid details and comic indignities. The winter landscape and weather are very strong here. The violence, when it comes, is unexpected and clumsy, without grandeur, like the violence we sometimes witness firsthand on the street.

Cogburn and LaBoeuf capture two shabby outlaws named Moon and Quincy, who know where Chaney is. They all sit together in a dark shack. Moon is wounded and wants to rat on Chaney.

"Don't act the fool!" said Quincy. "If you blow I will kill you."

But Moon went on. "I am played out," said he. "I must have a doctor. I will tell what I know."

With that, Quincy brought the bowie knife down on Moon's cuffed hand and chopped off four fingers which flew up before my eyes like chips from a log. Moon screamed and a rifle ball shattered the lantern in front of me and struck Quincy in the neck, causing hot blood to spurt on my face. My thought was: *I am better out of this.* I tumbled backward from the bench and sought a place of safety on the dirt floor.

The old-fashioned diction gives the scene the stiffness of a period illustration, but Portis can find poetic life inside the most wooden prose or dialogue.

Mattie tells us her story many years later, in 1928, when Al Smith is running for president. She is now a one-armed bank manager, hard as nails, and with no illusions about the people in town. "They love to slander you if you have any substance. They say I love nothing but money and the Presbyterian Church and that is why I never married. They think everybody is dying to get married." She never sees Cogburn again. When she learns he has died, she brings his body to town and buries him in the family plot with a good tombstone. She denies feeling anything but friendship for the man, but her denials are strangely moving. The final, deliberately flat-footed sentence is strangely moving, too. "This ends my true account of how I avenged Frank Ross's blood over in the Choctaw Nation when snow was on the ground."

This comic anti-western offers more excitement than most serious westerns. Cormac McCarthy looks phony by comparison. After you scrape off the fancy prose style, his novel *Blood Meridian* could be just the fantasy of a really mean adolescent boy who's seen too many Sergio Leone movies. But *True Grit,* with its mix of slapstick and bloodshed, toughness and tenderness, feels like the real thing.

The American West is a frequent setting for comedy, both fiction and nonfiction. Part of this is due to the influence of Mark Twain, whose voice haunts the region. But it's also due to the tradition of Western humor, which Twain refined and built upon. The wide-open spaces evoke a strange mix of jokey understatement and high exaggeration, a good language for laconic yarn-spinning. Many fine writers draw upon this language, most notably Larry McMurtry. But one of my favorite examples is Thomas Berger in his wonderful 1964 novel, *Little Big Man.*

While *True Grit* works in the backyard of old movies, *Little Big Man* works in the backyard of actual American history. This sprawling comic picaresque incorporates famous events and figures, including Wild Bill Hickok, Walt Whitman, and our old friend George Armstrong Custer. It's the first-person account of a 111-year-old man, Jack Crabb, spoken into a historian's tape recorder in 1952. Jack is a Huck Finn who has grown up and grown old and seen the country grow old around him. It's a sadder, wiser, richer voice.

Jack was captured by the Cheyenne when he was ten years old and spent the next five years as an Indian in a small band led by a chief named Old Lodge Skins. They call the short redhead with freckles Little Big Man. For the rest of his life, Jack goes back and forth between the world of whites and the world of the Cheyenne, never entirely at home in either. He sees both with a satirical eye. This is his description of the Cheyenne's war with another tribe, the Crow.

> When the Cheyenne gave the beating there was cele-
> bration. If it happened near our camp, the women
> and children went out and clubbed and stabbed the
> enemy wounded who was lying about and mutilated
> the dead, taking as souvenirs such items as noses,
> ears, and private parts. This was a real treat for them.
> If you seen as much as I did, you would have like me
> developed a strong stomach. Buffalo Wallow Woman
> was sort of my Ma, just a fine soul. I can't count all
> the times she hugged me against her fat belly . . . But
> now what'd you think when you saw that sweet per-
> son ripping open some helpless Crow with her knife
> and unwinding his guts?

One of the achievements of this novel is that the Indians are as strange and comic and real as the whites. Old Lodge Skins himself is a great comic character, ab-surd one moment, profound the next, transcending all easy judgments. He can be as racist as any white—the

Cheyenne call themselves "the Human Beings"—yet he begins in amused tolerance. He tells Jack:

> "Whatever else you can say about the white man, it must be admitted that *you cannot get rid of him.* He is in never-ending supply. There has always been only a limited number of Human Beings, because we are intended to be special and superior. Obviously not everybody can be a Human Being. To make this so, there must be a great many inferior people. To my mind, this is the function of the white men in the world. Therefore we must survive, because without us the world would not make sense."

But the next time Jack sees him, after the massacre at Sand Creek, where Old Lodge Skins loses his eyesight and two of his wives, the old man has stopped being amused by "Americans."

> "I no longer believe they are fools or crazy . . . The Human Beings believe that everything is alive: not only men and animals but also water and earth and stones and also the dead . . . But white men believe that everything is dead: stones, earth, animals, and people, even their own people. And if, in spite of that, things persist in trying to live, white men will rub them out."

Jack's own voice is loose and fluent. Unlike Mattie's slightly wooden written sentences, Jack's spoken sentences flow easily, mixing slang and bad grammar and five-dollar words. He is an excellent storyteller who makes his experience very real, both physically and emotionally. He shows us the intense darkness of the interior of a tepee after the bright sunlight outside. He compares the different smells of an Indian village and a white settlement, admitting he can grow accustomed to both but is startled by each when he's been living in the other. And he explores the very different attitudes about sex and violence among whites and Cheyenne. He is remarkably evenhanded. There are good whites, just as there are bad Indians, but he gives everybody valid reasons for doing what they do. (One trait that whites and Indians share is a mulish inability to listen to another person. More than once Jack must pull out a knife before the other person will understand what he's been saying for the past five minutes.)

Jack lives a remarkably varied life with an impressive range of roles in the white world: schoolboy, teamster, storekeeper, drunk, gambler, buffalo hunter, and scout. He has and loses two different families, one Cheyenne and one white. He is a resilient, flexible man who quickly adapts to whatever situation he's in, but the past frequently catches up with him. And there are horrors he cannot shake.

The novel's climax is the Battle of the Little Bighorn, and Jack's account is as brutal as Evan Connell's in *Son of the Morning Star.* It's fascinating to revisit the battle from a single point of view, albeit fictional, after experiencing it from the multiple points of view of Connell's history (which was published twenty years *after* Berger's novel). Because it's fiction, Berger can give us something the historians can't, a report of the massacre as experienced by the soldiers, including a final glimpse of Custer. Jack accompanies the Seventh Cavalry as a kind of court jester and is trapped on the hill with Custer and his men when they are overwhelmed by the Sioux and Cheyenne.

> I says: "General, won't you get down?"... He stared back with eyes like blue gems through the dust on his countenance, fanatic as an idol, and he says: "Splendid, boys! We have them on the run now!" And he went along the skirmish line, kicking the troopers' boots in encouragement, only some of them covered the feet of dead men.

The possibility is raised that Jack is a liar and the whole book is made up. But I believe Jack's story. He may stretch things now and then, but his tales are full of realistic grace notes and unpredictability, and they line up with the historical facts. Yes, Berger made it all up, of course, but if he wanted us to doubt Jack, he would've dropped a few obvious whoppers into his saga. And Jack's life story isn't nearly as interesting as a fantasy as it is as truth. As Jack says earlier, "I'm telling the truth here, and the truth is always made up of little particulars which sound ridiculous when repeated."

The novel ends with Jack back with the Cheyenne in the tepee of Old Lodge Skins. The old man is pleased his adopted son survived the battle; he doesn't need to know why he was with the whites. His first question is "Do you want to eat?"

Comedy can take us into tragedy—the destruction of the American Indian—and out again. The slapstick adds to the sorrow. This is a comic novel about genocide, but comedy opens the reader to a more complex and profound sadness than tragedy does, in part because we don't see sorrow coming.

Endings

In the last chapter of Philip Gourevitch's book on geno-cide in Rwanda, *We Wish to Inform You That Tomorrow We Will Be Killed with Our Families,* he shows how the first wave of murders was followed by a second wave when survivors sought revenge. Just when the reader be-gins to fear the killing will never end, a weary coworker comes upon Gourevitch reading a novel. "Novels are nice," says the coworker. "They stop."

Because history doesn't stop. It keeps happening. "Success is never final," said Winston Churchill. But neither is defeat—sometimes. William Dean Howells claimed that Americans want tragedies with happy endings, which history can actually produce if given enough time. But, as we've seen, history can also pro-duce comedies with *unhappy* endings.

When writing any story, fiction or nonfiction, it is hard to know where to stop. A novel that ends with a marriage will tell one story. One that ends with the divorce a few years later tells another. A work of his-tory that ends with the surrender at Appomattox is a triumphant story of emancipation and reunion. One that ends twelve years after that, with the collapse of Reconstruction, is a sad tale of corruption and defeat.

The writer must choose an ending, since endlessness is akin to shapelessness, and a run-on story can be as annoying as a run-on sentence. But sometimes a writer will discover a new truth by staying on the train long after it's passed its expected destination.

A fascinating example of this is *The Unredeemed Captive* by John Demos. This is the story of a 1704 raid on Deerfield, Massachusetts, and its aftermath. One hundred and twelve men, women, and children were captured by a band of French and Indians and carried back to Canada over the snow and ice. With them were their minister, John Williams, his wife, his nine-year-old son Stephen, and his seven-year-old daughter Eunice. The wife was killed along the way because she was too weak to travel. Over the next few years, the captives were ransomed (redeemed) and returned home—all but Eunice. She remained with a band of Christian Mohawks, the Kahnawakes, also known as Praying Indians or Praying Iroquois. Not even the French could arrange her release, although she was held in a village just across the river from Montreal. This is a captivity story, a nonfiction precursor to *Little Big Man,* but in another part of the continent and 150 years earlier. Like Jack Crabb, the captive happily joined the tribe.

Francis Parkman told the same tale in *France and England in North America* in a highly readable twenty-five pages. Demos digs deeper. An academic historian whose books include a study of New England witch-craft, *Entertaining Satan,* which mixes psychology and social history, Demos aims for something different in *Captive.* "Most of all, I wanted to write a *story,*" he begins. He opens with multiple beginnings, ranging from the birth of Eunice Williams to the death of Charles II of Spain (which led to the War of the Spanish Succession, which crossed the ocean to produce the attack on Deerfield). Demos keeps the strange spellings and punctuation of the original documents, and his book is not always an easy read—he must frequently translate for the reader. But his approach keeps the past strange and exotic, a mystery to be explored from the present. This is a detective story as well as a historical narrative.

As soon as John Williams was free, he wrote a short book with a long title: *The Redeemed Captive Returning to Zion: A Faithful History of Remarkable Occurrences in the Captivity and Deliverance of Mr. John Williams, Minister of the Gospel, in Deerfield, Who, in the Desolation, Which Befell That Plantation, by an Incursion of the French and Indians, Was by Them Carried Away with His Family and His Neighborhood unto Canada.* Full of God, guilt, and divine providence, it became a Puritan best seller. Meanwhile he and others wrote letters to the French Canadians, trying to arrange for the return of his missing daughter.

Eunice disappears for years into Mohawk life. Then,

in 1712, when she is only fifteen, word comes that she has married "a Philistine"—a Catholic Indian. A cousin shares his horror in a letter:

> I Conclude you had before Us The Melancholy News Concerning Cousen Eunice Which I hope We have still Grounds to hope is Not True, & Must Still pray In Faith for her redemption, May I Not Say as Was said to Monica The Mother of Augustine, That a Child of So Many Prayers Cant be Lost . . .

Her conversion to Catholicism is as shocking to the family as her marriage to an Indian.

After the war finally ends, a few New Englanders visit Eunice, including her own father. They report that she has forgotten her English but says little to them in any language. Eunice is silent throughout this narrative, and Demos briefly resorts to speculative fiction at one point to see things from her point of view.

John Williams dies in 1729, but the story keeps going, which is where it gets stranger and more interesting. Eunice shows up in Albany with her Mohawk husband, Arosen, in 1740. She meets her brother Stephen, now a minister. He keeps a long diary, but it's one of the most frustrating sources imaginable. All he says of the encounter is that it's a "joyfull, Sorrowfull meeting of our poor Sister yt we had been Sepratd from fer above

36 years." Again Demos must fill the gap with a speculative account. The second half of the story, the silent half, cries out for a novelist, but Demos gains something by remaining true to the dense resistance of mute history. It has a weight and mystery no novel could achieve.

The reunion of the brother and sister would make a good ending for a novel, but the story keeps going. Eunice and her husband visit her brother four times over the years, including a visit during the Great Awakening, New England's time of religious conversion. They sit silently in church while another minister delivers a sermon on the captivity of sin, comparing it to the "Thickness of popish Darkness & Superstition" that Eunice experiences. Eunice disappears again during the French and Indian War, the American name for the Seven Years' War that made life so miserable for Madame de Pompadour. She reappears one last time in the form of a dictated letter to her brother in 1771—the closest we come to hearing her voice.

The brother and sister both lived remarkably long lives. Stephen died at age eighty-nine, in 1782, followed by Eunice, also at eighty-nine, in 1785, after the end of the Revolutionary War. But the story *still* doesn't end. Her great-grandson passed himself off as the last of the Bourbons, the Lost Dauphin, Louis XVII. Again, truth is stranger than fiction, but this tale later inspired the subplot of a novel, the Duke and Dauphin episodes in *Huckleberry Finn.*

Demos patiently, doggedly follows a tale long past the point when most storytellers would've quit. The sources are sparse, and we're left with more questions than answers. Yet he takes us on an exciting journey up a mountain trail into the high, thin air of a past imperfect where we can cross over into different cultures and eras.

Novels have learned from history: they don't always stop, either. They go for realism by adding epilogues and then give the epilogues their own epilogues. *The Leopard* properly ends with the death of the Prince, but two epilogue chapters follow, showing the decline of the family into religious superstition and shabby gentility. *The Assault* by Harry Mulisch opens with a terrible episode in Holland during the Nazi occupation, when a Dutch family is executed in reprisal for an assassination. Only the twelve-year-old son, Anton, survives. The rest of this succinct, heartfelt 192-page novel is all epilogues—four, in fact—as we move from 1945 to 1981, learning how Anton deals with his trauma. The book is not strictly a historical novel, since the protagonist is the same age as Mulisch, yet it works as recent history, showing how people outlive their past but still carry it with them.

I am very fond of epilogues myself. Draper accuses me of suffering from separation anxiety: I do not want to say good-bye to my characters. That's probably true, but I also think my love of epilogues comes from my reading of history: I know the story will continue.

So, how do writers find the right ending? I could just quote the King's advice from *Alice's Adventures in Wonderland:* "Begin at the beginning and go on till you come to the end: then stop." But we often find the ending only by trial and error.

I tried an epilogue with my novel *Father of Frankenstein,* but I couldn't make it work. The novel proper ends with the death of James Whale. I jumped ahead ten years to show Clay Boone, the gardener, now married and with a family, watching *Bride of Frankenstein* on late night TV with his son. But it fell flat. I needed to start the story all over again, and the epilogue gave the story too many extra beats, like a bouncing ball that won't stop bouncing. When Bill Condon adapted my book into his movie *Gods and Monsters,* I told him about my cut epilogue, and he had a go at it. And he made it fly. Film is quicker than prose—you don't need to explain or convince the reader; you just show the next scene. Condon gave the episode what I couldn't find, an emotional payoff. Readers and viewers can put up with a few extra bounces so long as the ball lands somewhere interesting. And Condon did it very simply: Clay takes out the garbage and walks like the Monster in the rain. With a little help from the music, we *see* Clay remembering his dead friend.

Talk of epilogues brings us back to *War and Peace*. The book is famous for its epilogues. Despite its glories and pleasures, for many readers this is the novel that refuses to end.

Tolstoy begins with the First Epilogue, a brisk set of pages that takes the surviving characters through seven years of marriages, births, and the paying of debts, until they all come together on a winter night in 1820. He follows this with the notorious Second Epilogue, where he crosses the border from fiction into history, and not just history but a philosophy of history. He is so proud of what he's accomplished that he believes the novel must mean more: he has somehow solved history. Meaning for Tolstoy is the ultimate ending of his novel.

The Second Epilogue is less than fifty pages long, but it feels interminable. We shift from the novelist's world of specifics—bodies and emotions and acts—to an amateur philosopher's jumble of ideas. Tolstoy asks some good questions. Has history replaced God? What moves nations? Do historians really know anything? But his answers are airy and contradictory. This is not the good, gritty nineteenth-century history of Macaulay and Parkman but the gassy spirit history of Hegel and Carlyle.

Tolstoy argues that the individual is helpless within the cosmic machinery of history. Even leaders are helpless. There's a good analogy about the beasts in the front of the herd only appearing to lead the herd. This dismissal of leaders is the result of Tolstoy reducing Napoleon to a nullity, a figurehead, a mascot of history. We can't blame Tolstoy for being disappointed by Napoleon. He's one of those figures from the past whose fame and grandeur puzzle the present. For many of us he's just a short, grumpy dictator in a harlequin hat. (Some historians now argue that he wasn't really so short.) Yet most historians, and most novelists, too, give Bonaparte more weight than Tolstoy allows him. He genuinely believes Napoleon is too unimportant to have produced the massive movement of armies in 1812. He knows this leaves a giant hole in the story. So what produced these events; what drove the train? Tolstoy thinks that if he can find the answer, he can discover the real laws of historical action. He suggests the solution might be in economics but admits the science isn't there yet.

He leaves the question unanswered and spends the rest of the Second Epilogue arguing with himself about free will and determinism. Man is free as an individual but completely determined inside the larger actions of history. Like anyone arguing with himself, and like his fictional characters, Tolstoy often contradicts himself. He insists there must be general laws of history but is scornful of any historian who claims to have found them. The common reader usually gives up here, but a few critics dig deeper, hoping to find the real meaning of *War and Peace.* The most famous is Isaiah Berlin, who, in "The Hedgehog and the Fox," popularized an intriguing Greek saying ("The fox knows many things, but the hedgehog knows one big thing") but is not very helpful about the novel. Among other points, he claims that Tolstoy meant to say that determinism works at all levels of human activity, the historical *and* the individual, but that's not true.

Tolstoy argues with hypothetical historians for two dozen pages before concluding that a belief in free will has confused the study of history just as a belief that the earth was the center of the universe confused astronomy for centuries. Well, maybe, but what does that mean? And how does it translate to the experience of Pierre, Natasha, and the others?

These pages are not the real point of the novel, Tolstoy's original purpose in writing it. He didn't start adding his reflections on history until he was working on the second half of the book. Some of the earlier two- and three-page digressions are interesting; the rest are irrelevant. Before Tolstoy gets to the Second Epilogue, he's said everything that's useful. But he could not let go. Curiously, he removed the Second Epilogue from the 1873 edition, at the same time that he translated all the French dialogue into Russian. The book is better without it. His wife reinstated it in the 1886 edition, presumably with his approval.

The useful comments about history are all scattered earlier in the novel. Here he establishes the two realms of private life and the hive life of history. "There are two sides to life for every individual: a personal life, in which his freedom exists in proportion to the abstract nature of his interests, and an elemental life within the swarm of humanity, in which a man inevitably follows laws laid down for him." (Tolstoy doesn't write about ideas half as clearly as he writes about his fictional characters.) He argues that the higher up one goes in the chain of command, the more a person is bound by circumstance. Enlisted men and peasants are more free than their leaders. "Kings are the slaves of history."

Later he turns to calculus in his search for historical meaning. "Only by adopting an infinitely small unit for observation, the differential in history otherwise known as human homogeneity, and perfecting the art of integration (the adding up of infinitesimals) can we have any hope of determining the laws of history." I don't know about the laws of history, but I believe that this "small unit for observation" is the proper scale for writing about history. What he describes sounds like the human scale, which is the scale of novels. It's the scale in which Tolstoy successfully works for more than a thousand pages, but he has lost faith in his accomplishment by the time he writes his conclusion.

The truth of *War and Peace*—the key truth of many novels about history—lies in its examples of individual men and women trying to find the room to be human inside the dense, elaborate machinery of history. They want the breathing space of private life. It's what Sethe finally finds in *Beloved* and the Prince anxiously sustains in *The Leopard*. It's what Sergey Nabokov loses in *The Unreal Life of Sergey Nabokov* and the two lovers achieve at the close of *Love in the Time of Cholera*. As readers, we often go to history to escape the confines of our private lives, but once there we read about characters who yearn to escape history, to go back into the private and personal.

The real ending of Tolstoy's novel comes in the First Epilogue. Natasha, Pierre, Nikolay, and Marya all survive the war. The two families gather at the Bolkonsky estate on a snowy night after Pierre's return from Moscow. Tempers and egos show, but these people are genuinely fond of one another; they've found a plausible happiness in private life. We catch some of this happiness in the wonderful scene where Pierre and Natasha talk in bed:

> The moment they were alone together Natasha too began to converse with her husband in that manner peculiar to husbands and wives, one of those in which ideas are perceived and exchanged with extraordinary clarity and speed by some means that transcends all the rules of logic and develops its own way without any spoken assertions, deductions or conclusions. Natasha was so used to talking to her husband like this that she took any process of logical thinking on Pierre's part as an unmistakable sign that something was wrong between them.

Pierre has secretly met with people who want to save Russia from the tsar. Natasha disapproves. She knows, like Tolstoy, that there is no happiness in the public sphere of politics.

Downstairs, in his own bed, little Nikolay Bolkonsky, the orphaned son of Prince Andrey, is asleep, dreaming of going into battle alongside Uncle Pierre, leading an army of white gossamer threads against another gossamer army, finding glory in a battle with cobwebs. "Everybody will know me and love me and admire me," he thinks.

The entire novel is an argument against the delusions

of fame and power. The individual is a creature of no importance in the great scheme of things. History is a trap; history is trouble. All that matters is private happiness. Yet Tolstoy, the sad realist, ends the book with a young boy dreaming of glory and fame and the temptations of history.

Author's Note

I have many people to thank for this book. First there is Charles Baxter, who suggested I take on this project. He somehow knew that I was a good match for the subject, something he recognized before I did. He provided valuable advice and ideas along the way.

Good friends also helped me. Bob Smith is not only a wonderful writer and stand-up comic but also a very wise reader of history. Damien Jack, James Goodman, and my partner, Draper Shreeve, all offered examples, criticism, and encouragement. And my physician, Dr. Michael Matarese, a lover of American and military history, happily shared titles while I sat on his examining table. (He fervently disagrees with me about *The Killer Angels*.)

Steve Woodward at Graywolf gave excellent suggestions and support at the end. Associate publisher Katie Dublinski and our copyeditor Katharine Cooper were wonderful to work with.

But I most want to thank Barbara Chalmers MacEdwards, my grandmother. Gramma Mac was a painter and bookkeeper who was also a keen reader. She left her intellectual and artistic stamp on all seven of her grandchildren. She fed my history addiction as a boy with good books and smart questions and a subscription to *American Heritage* magazine. Born in 1906, the daughter of a Congregationalist minister, she was a living bridge to the past. I dedicate this book to her memory.

Books Referred To and Recommended

Little Big Man by Thomas Berger

The Ordeal of Elizabeth Marsh by Linda Colley

Son of the Morning Star by Evan S. Connell

The Unredeemed Captive by John Demos

Love in the Time of Cholera by Gabriel García Márquez

Incidents in the Life of a Slave Girl by Harriet Jacobs

Middle Passage by Charles Johnson

Black Masters by Michael P. Johnson and James L. Roark

History of England by Thomas Babington Macaulay

The Path between the Seas by David McCullough

Madame de Pompadour by Nancy Mitford

Benjamin Franklin by Edmund Morgan

Beloved by Toni Morrison

The Assault by Harry Mulisch

France and England in North America by Francis Parkman

True Grit by Charles Portis

The Fabulous History of the Dismal Swamp Company
   by Charles Royster

The Unreal Life of Sergey Nabokov by Paul Russell

Pickett's Charge by George R. Stewart

Eminent Victorians by Lytton Strachey

The Confessions of Nat Turner by William Styron

The Internal Enemy by Alan Taylor

War and Peace by Leo Tolstoy

The Leopard by Giuseppe Tomasi di Lampedusa

Burr by Gore Vidal

Ecstatic Nation by Brenda Wineapple

Orlando by Virginia Woolf

Mr. Mani by A. B. Yehoshua

Harriet Jacobs: A Life by Jean Fagan Yellin

CHRISTOPHER BRAM is the author of nine novels, including *Gods and Monsters* (formerly titled *Father of Frankenstein*), and two previous works of nonfiction, *Eminent Outlaws* and *Mapping the Territory.* He has received a Guggenheim Fellowship and the Bill Whitehead Award for Lifetime Achievement. He lives in Greenwich Village and teaches at the Gallatin School of New York University.

The text of *The Art of History* is set in Warnock Pro, a typeface designed by Robert Slimbach for Adobe Systems in 2000. Book design by Wendy Holdman. Composition by Bookmobile Design & Digital Publisher Services, Minneapolis, Minnesota. Manufactured by Versa Press on acid-free, 30 percent postconsumer wastepaper.